D0931876

CASE STUDIES IN

CULTURAL ANTHROPOLOGY

GENERAL EDITORS

George and Louise Spindler

STANFORD UNIVERSITY

———————

THE HURON

Farmers of the North

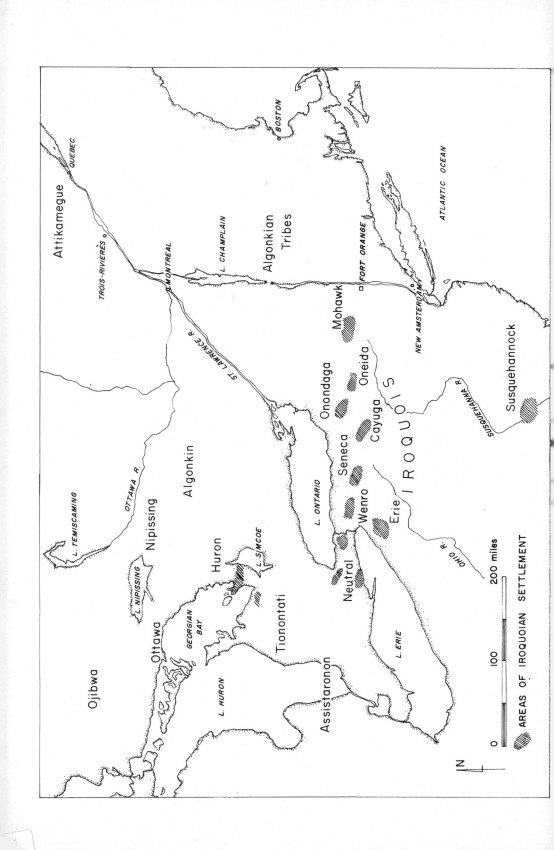

AREAS OF IROQUOIAN SETTLEMENT

THE HURON

Farmers of the North

By

BRUCE G. TRIGGER
McGill University

HOLT, RINEHART AND WINSTON

NEW YORK   CHICAGO   SAN FRANCISCO   ATLANTA

DALLAS   MONTREAL   TORONTO   LONDON   SYDNEY

Cover picture: Carved bone figure from historic Huron site. Length: 3½ inches.

Library of Congress Catalog Card Number: 77–92315
ISBN: 0–03–0796550–8
Printed in the United States of America
23456 059 987654

To Barbara

Foreword

About the Series

These case studies in cultural anthropology are designed to bring to students, in beginning and intermediate courses in the social sciences, insights into the richness and complexity of human life as it is lived in different ways and in different places. They are written by men and women who have lived in the societies they write about and who are professionally trained as observers and interpreters of human behavior. The authors are also teachers, and in writing their books they have kept the students who will read them foremost in their minds. It is our belief that when one gains an understanding of ways of life very different from one's own, abstractions and generalizations about social structure, cultural values, subsistence techniques, and the other universal categories of human social behavior become meaningful.

About the Author

Bruce G. Trigger is currently Professor of Anthropology at McGill University in Montreal, Canada. He was born in Preston, Ontario, in 1937 and obtained his B.A. degree from the University of Toronto and his Ph.D. from Yale University. Professor Trigger has carried out archaeological research in Egypt and the Sudan, and his interest in the ethnohistory of eastern North America dates from his undergraduate days at Toronto. He is a fellow of the Royal Anthropological Institute, the American Anthropological Association, and Sigma Xi. His publications include three books, *History and Settlement in Lower Nubia* (1965), *The Late Nubian Settlement at Arminna West* (1967), and *Beyond History: The Methods of Prehistory* (1968), as well as numerous articles dealing with Sudanese prehistory, Iroquoian ethnohistory, and archaeological theory. He is the recipient of a Canada Council Leave Fellowship for the academic year 1968–1969, which will enable him to begin work on a major study of Franco-Huron relations from a Huron point of view.

About the Book

Despite the vast historical and ethnographic literature on the American Indian, there are surprisingly few well-rounded descriptive analyses of tribal cultures as functioning systems. This relative lack results in part from the fact that professional anthropologists met the Indians late in the life span of the latter's cultures. With the exception of some far northern and southwestern peoples, their cultures were usually so fragmented that their elements could be described, but the traditional culture as a coherent way of life could not, excepting as a memory culture. In addition, until very recently, anthropologists did not feel it worthwhile to describe most contemporary Indian communities since they were almost always perceived as disintegrated, culturally impoverished, and maladapted.

It is with special delight that one encounters a lively, at times anecdotal, and relatively complete account of a culture whose bearers virtually became extinct more than three hundred years ago. In this case study the Huron, an Iroquoian people of great significance in the cultural development of aboriginal North America and in the early phase of European and Indian contact, come to life once again.

Utilizing a wide variety of historical sources and interpretations, Bruce Trigger has produced a synthesis that gives us a remarkably coherent picture of an extinct culture as a working system. This culture is remarkable even without the added luster of time. A sedentary, agricultural but warlike people, the Hurons maintained their society with social and political controls that were complex and based upon rational discussion and judgment, as well as upon belief and sentiment. Particularly impressive are the culturally patterned techniques in Huron culture for maintaining individual balance. The culture provided channels through which the idiosyncratic needs of individuals could be met, sometimes in a spectacular manner and often in ways that transgressed normal sanctions on behavior. As a participant-observer in our own society and times, one views the inventions by others for the maintenance of psychic security and personal satisfaction with special interest. One glimpses, in this setting, some of the weaknesses of human nature and culturally patterned devices for the support of the shaky human ego. In this context one is left awed and depressed by the torture and murder of captives by the Hurons. The ability of man to perceive other people, even those virtually identical to him in race and culture, as objects, while thinking of himself and his cohorts as human, is seen clearly in this behavior. Sadly, one sees also that this very ability, especially in the context of a rationally organized, even, one might say, a psychiatrically sophisticated society, functions to help define the boundaries of good and bad, real and illusory, and gives validity to actions and belief within those boundaries. We may see in Huron culture, as remote in time and origin from our own as it is, a reflection of our common and contemporary problems. The Hurons solved these problems in their own unique manner, but in ways recognizable to us.

GEORGE AND LOUISE SPINDLER
General Editors

Portola Valley, Calif.
July 1969

Preface

When I was asked to write this book, my first reaction was negative. Elisabeth Tooker's *An Ethnography of the Huron Indians* had appeared only two years before and another work on Huron ethnography seemed superfluous.

The fact that I have written this book does not indicate any dissatisfaction with Dr. Tooker's monograph, which I continue to regard as an extremely important and lasting contribution to Iroquoian studies. Rather, it reflects a growing conviction that the rich data concerning the Huron are far from exhausted and that a study of these data from a somewhat different point of view will complement rather than duplicate Tooker's work.

In *An Ethnography of the Huron Indians,* Elisabeth Tooker set out to gather together in a single easily accessible volume all of the available ethnographic data pertaining to the Huron. This task she accomplished in an admirable fashion; her book is an indispensable sourcework which I am convinced can never be bettered. In addition, she compared these data with what is known about the cognate Iroquois and Wyandot peoples.

Dr. Tooker approached the Huron from the point of view of someone who had worked among the Iroquois and was familiar with their culture. My own background is different, my interest in Huron culture having grown out of an interest in the prehistory of Ontario. First, it seemed to me that this difference in orientation might permit me to treat the Huron in a different manner from Tooker. Secondly, I felt that there was need to view Huron culture as a working system and to concentrate on the interrelationships among its parts rather than attempting to trace the relationship between the various aspects of Huron culture and their analogues among the Iroquois. It is principally these functional and historical interests that distinguish the present book from Tooker's ethnography.

I would like to stress that this study is an historical ethnography. It is therefore necessarily based on fieldwork done by people other than the author. Because of this, data are not always as abundant as one might wish, and they are not always available on topics of one's choosing. This considerably increases the difficulties of any functional analysis. In spite of this, one of the delights of this study has been the realization of how essentially similar are the techniques that historians and ethnographers utilize in analyzing their respective data. I have chosen to treat the written sources as oral informants and therefore have omitted a plethora of footnotes documenting the various statements I have made concerning Huron culture. Those interested in tracing the sources of any particular statement can easily do so through Tooker's Huron ethnography, which they should learn to use as the basic sourcebook on Huron culture.

I wish to thank Mrs. Susan Weeks for preparing the frontispiece and Figs. 1 (below), 3, and 5. Figure 1 (above) was supplied courtesy of the Public

Archives, Ottawa. Figures 2, 4, 6, 7, and 8 are reproduced from Champlain, *Voyages et descouvertures faites en la Nouvelle France* 1619, and Fig. 9 is from Lafitau, *Moeurs des Sauvages,* 1724. These are taken from originals in the Repath Library, McGill University. The cover illustration is reproduced from James B. Griffin's *Archeology of the Eastern United States* with the kind permission of Kenneth E. Kidd and the University of Chicago Press. I wish to thank Miss Evelyn Weinreb for typing the manuscript. The cost of secretarial services and obtaining illustrations was met by a grant from the Humanities and Social Sciences Research Fund, McGill University. The book was completed while I was a recipient of a Canada Council Leave Fellowship.

Finally, I wish to dedicate this book to my wife, Barbara, as a wedding present.

BRUCE G. TRIGGER

London, England
July 1969

Contents

$\boxed{1}$

Introduction

I N 1650 weeds grew in the cornfields of the Huron. Two years before children
had played in front of the houses; now there was silence. Abandoned
hearths, charred poles, and rotting slabs of cedar bark were all that remained of
a series of villages that had once been inhabited by over 20,000 people.

About thirty-five years earlier, the French had begun to visit the four
tribes they called the Huron. They had found their settlements strewn across a
small peninsula located between Georgian Bay and Lake Simcoe, in southern
Ontario. The prosperity of the Huron was unmatched by that of any of the other
tribes the French had encountered along the Saint Lawrence River or in Ontario.
Their populous villages, often surrounded with palisades, were larger and more
stable than the encampments of the nomadic peoples who inhabited the rocky,
lake-covered regions to the north, an area rich in fish and game, but little suited
for agriculture. The rolling hills of Huronia supported a prosperous horticultural
economy, and the Huron were accustomed to trade their surplus produce with
the Algonkian hunters of the north.

For a brief period in the first half of the seventeenth century the Huron
played a key role in the history of eastern North America (Trigger 1960, 1965,
1968). Because of their connections with the tribes who lived in the vicinity of
the Upper Great Lakes, they were able to supply the French with vast quantities
of beaver pelts. In return, the Huron secured European kettles, knives, and
hatchets, which they recognized as superior to their own, as well as beads and
other trinkets, all of which were much desired by themselves and by neighboring
tribes.

Between 1610 and 1650 numerous explorers, traders, and missionaries
made the hazardous journey inland to conclude treaties with the Huron, encourage
them to trade, and save their souls. Unlike most modern anthropologists, these
visitors did not find themselves living among a people who had long been influenced
by European ways and who lived under the surveillance and control of a colonial
administration that had altered their way of life according to European standards

1

of propriety. On the contrary, they became the guests of a people over whom they had no political control and among whom the Jesuits were unable to exercise any significant influence before 1645. In this exotic cultural environment, individual Frenchmen found themselves alternately scandalized, repelled, and fascinated by the behavior of a people who were uninfluenced by beliefs and standards they themselves had never questioned. Many came to know the Huron well and developed at least a working understanding of the principles upon which their culture was based. The vivid accounts of Huron life that some of these men recorded serve as the basis for our understanding of the Huron confederacy.

Unfortunately, these same Europeans unwittingly helped to set in motion a chain of events that was to destroy the Huron and many neighboring peoples. Unfamiliar diseases, such as measles and smallpox, were carried from the French settlements into the interior. As a result, thousands of Indians died and many tribes vanished as distinctive entities. Moreover, as beaver became exhausted in upper New York State, the Iroquois, who traded with the Dutch along the Hudson River, began to seek a share of the furs that the Huron were obtaining from the north. This gradually transformed a traditional feud with the Huron into a bloody war. In the course of this war the Iroquois, who were able to secure more guns than were their rivals, gradually gained the upper hand (Tooker 1963).

In the spring of 1649, after suffering a series of defeats of unprecedented severity, the Huron decided that their situation had become untenable and abandoned their villages. Many perished at the hands of Iroquois scalping parties and from famine and privations; others found refuge among neighboring tribes. A large number ended up living with the Iroquois, who welcomed them as a means of increasing their own numbers. Most of the latter settled in existing communities, but the smallest Huron tribe, the Tahontaenrat, along with some of the Ahrendar-rhonon, were allowed to build a new village, called Gandougarse, in the tribal territory of the Seneca. In time, however, all of the Huron who joined the Iroquois lost their sense of ethnic identity and identified themselves with their conquerors.

About three-hundred Huron Christians, the survivors of a far larger number of people that spent the winter of 1649–1650 living on Gahendoe (Christian) Island off the coast of Huronia, settled under French protection on the Isle d'Orleans, near Quebec City. Six years later they were transferred to the mainland, where they continue to live today. These people have retained their identity as Hurons, but have intermarried extensively with the French settlers; they ceased speaking Huron about a century ago.

Many of the Huron, particularly from the Attignawantan or Bear tribe, sought refuge among the Tionontati, a people who lived west of Huronia along the south shore of Georgian Bay and whose language and culture were similar to those of the Huron. Soon, however, the Tionontati, together with these Huron refugees, were driven out of southern Ontario by the Iroquois, who did not wish to see the Huron trade fall into the hands of yet another tribe. Although mostly Tionontati, the survivors, about eight hundred in number, came to be known as the Wyandot, a corruption of *Wendat*, the former name for the Huron confederacy. For fifty years the Wyandot lived in the region of the Upper Great Lakes, and were divided into several bands, each containing only a few hundred people. During this period they had close contacts with the Ottawa, Potawatomi, and other Algonkian-speaking tribes who lived in this area, and their culture was much influenced by them. In 1701 the French persuaded the Wyandot to settle close to Fort Pontchartrain, which was being built near Detroit. Today, some of the descendants of the Wyandot live near Sandwich, Ontario, the rest on the Wyandotte Reservation in Oklahoma. Both groups have abandoned their native language, although it was still spoken at the turn of the century (Barbeau 1960).

With the rapid development of an interest in the history of North America that took place in the nineteenth century, the Huron suffered the final misfortune of the vanquished: They became the victims of romantic fables. Historians who were impressed by the success that the Jesuit missionaries had among them contrasted the assumed docility and peaceableness of the Huron with the blood-thirsty ferocity of the Iroquois. Other historians attributed the downfall of the Huron to their cowardice and contrasted their "disorganization" and "love of trade" with the aggressiveness and hardy discipline of their foes. Such myths obscured rather than explained the Huron and their culture. The aim of the present book is to ignore these myths and to describe Huron culture as it appeared when it was first observed by the French.

Informants

Our ethnographic information does not come from the Huron, who were nonliterate, but from Europeans who visited Huronia in the first half of the seventeenth century and wrote accounts of what they saw there. The historical anthropologist is at an obvious disadvantage because he is unable to observe first-hand the people he is studying. Nevertheless, when the written sources are abundant, he can treat them in much the same way that the ethnologist does his informants. Different statements can be cross-checked against one another and compared with what is known about the closely related Iroquois and Wyandot cultures at a later period. Finally, additional clues about Huron culture may be sought in the related fields of archaeology and linguistics. In this way it becomes possible to reconstruct a tolerably detailed picture of Huron life in the first half of the seventeenth century.

The information that we have about the Huron is unique; no other tribe in eastern North America having been described in such minute detail so soon after contact with the Europeans. Although the Iroquois have been studied in greater detail than the Huron, comparable data concerning their culture are not available until long after 1650. The curious juncture of colonial policy, trade, and missionary zeal that led to the documentation of the Huron has thus contributed significantly to our awareness of cultural diversity and cultural development in the northeastern woodlands.

The principal written sources of information about the Huron are three in number. The earliest is Samuel de Champlain's account of his visit to Huronia between August 1615 and May 1616. During this time he spent approximately five months living in a number of Huron villages. Champlain was a soldier, explorer, and cartographer who devoted the latter part of his life to supervising the development of the French colony along the Saint Lawrence River. He died commander of this colony in 1635. Prior to coming to Canada, Champlain had traveled in the West Indies and had acquired a first-hand knowledge of the Spanish colonies in the New World. From the beginning, he was aware that the fur trade was of paramount importance for the economic development of New France, and for this reason he sought to win the friendship and respect of the Algonkian-speaking tribes who lived in the fur-rich regions north of the Saint Lawrence and of their Huron allies. In order to do this he was willing to hunt with these Indians and to fight with them against their enemies.

Champlain not only was a skillful geographer but he also carefully observed the tribes he visited. While his account of the Huron is not particularly long, it provides us with a useful picture of their culture. Since Champlain was particularly interested in persuading the Huron chiefs to trade with the French, it is not surprising that the most successful portions of his account are those describing the Huron economy and interpersonal relations. As an unquestioning supporter of the French crown, Champlain judged very harshly any type of government or legal system that was different from those of France, dismissing it as being formless and chaotic. Champlain's strong religious convictions also led him to scorn Huron religion.

Our second informant is a man of completely different temperament. Gabriel Sagard, a Recollet friar, arrived in Huronia in August 1623 and lived there until May of the following year. Since it was impossible to convert the Huron, Sagard spent most of his time mastering their language and observing their customs. He published these observations in a book entitled *Le Grand Voyage du Pays des Hurons,* which rightly may be considered one of the world's earliest substantial ethnographies. In his book Sagard wrote up his observations concerning the plants, animals, and people of Huronia. Unlike Champlain, Sagard did not hunt or fight alongside the Huron (although he did accompany a fishing party to Georgian Bay), nor did he manage to visit more than a fraction of the country. Nevertheless, his account is unique. If many years of work in Huronia were to make the Jesuits more familiar with the details of Huron culture, none was to leave behind as careful a picture of everyday life as it was lived in an average Huron village. His dictionary or phrase list of the Huron language constitutes an additional source of information about Huron culture.

Our third source of information is *The Jesuit Relations and Allied Documents.* The *Relations,* which were published yearly in Paris, contain a chronicle of missionary activities among the Huron between the years 1634 and 1650. From 1635 to 1638 these reports were written by Fathers Jean de Brebeuf and François Joseph le Mercier. During the early years of their mission, the Jesuits were working hard to understand Huron culture, and their writings are filled with descriptions of Huron life. Brebeuf and Le Mercier both had temperaments that were well-suited to the difficult work of these years. Their writings reflect warm personal involvement with a people on whom their teachings as yet had little effect. Both men were also gifted writers, and their descriptions of Huron culture are often of superb quality.

In 1639, the writing of the Huron *Relations* was taken over by Father Jerome Lalemant, a new superior of the mission who had just arrived from France. Lalemant was a skillful administrator, but he lacked the personal warmth of his predecessors. He did not have as many personal dealings with the Huron and found their way of life dirty and unpalatable. In writing his annual report he devoted most of his attention to describing the growth of the Christian church in Huronia. The clash between Christian and native beliefs led him to be interested in only one aspect of traditional culture, Huron religious beliefs. His successor, Father Paul Ragueneau, continued to describe the development of the church and provided a vivid running account of the Iroquois attacks that finally destroyed the Huron confederacy. Ragueneau had a keen intelligence and superb critical faculties. Like Lalemant, he recorded much valuable information about Huron religion.

The Jesuit Relations are especially valuable because they represent a study in depth of Huron culture. Being well-trained scholars, the Jesuits were careful to record not only their general conclusions about the Huron but also many of the observations on which these conclusions were based. In spite of this, it is a mistake for the anthropologist to picture the Jesuits too much in his own image. The Jesuits were in Huronia to win converts, and their attempts to understand Huron culture were pragmatic ones largely directed toward this goal. It is significant that in spite of all the years the Jesuits were in Huronia they show no sign of having understood the difference between tribes, clans, and lineages, nor did they note that the Huron kinship system was different from their own. These concepts do not appear to have been sufficiently important in the Jesuits' dealings with the Huron that they were compelled to take note of them. Likewise, the Jesuits say practically nothing about Huron subsistence activities and very little about trade and warfare, except insofar as the latter activities provided them with the opportunity for making contact with other tribes. However, *The Jesuit Relations* provide much information about Huron law, government, and religion.

Some incidental information about Huron culture can be found in various letters written by men working in Huronia (Gendron 1660; Thwaites, *passim*), in Pierre Boucher's (1664) history of New France, in Father Pierre Chaumonot's autobiography, and in Father Francesco Bressani's Italian synopsis of the Jesuit writings concerning the Huron.

It is important to note that all of our major sources of information about the Huron were popular works designed to acquaint readers in France with what was going on in the New World and to elicit their support. They were works of propaganda first and works of history only second. The Jesuits certainly collected a great deal more information about the Huron than they chose to record in their annual relations. They refer, for example, to Huron historical traditions that they left unrecorded, apparently for fear of boring the reader. There is now no hope of those traditions being recovered. In spite of such shortcomings, the writings of Champlain, Sagard, and the Jesuits make available a wealth of information that would otherwise have been lost to us.

2

The Land and the People

THE HURON called themselves the Wendat, a term generally believed to mean "Islanders" or "Dwellers in a Peninsula." This term has been interpreted as referring to the large bodies of water that surround the Huron country on three sides, but it may also reflect the Huron belief that the world was an island supported on the back of a turtle.[1] The term Huron is derived from the French word *hure* meaning, literally, a boar, but more generally a ruffian or savage.

The Huron, like most of the tribes in southern Ontario and upper New York State, spoke one of the related languages that linguists classify as Iroquoian, a term not to be confused with Iroquois. The latter is an Algonkian word commonly used by the French and English to refer to the five nations of New York State, all of whom were Iroquoian-speaking. The Iroquoian languages of the Northeast are distantly related to Cherokee, spoken in the southern Appalachians, and to Tuscarora, spoken nearer the coast in North Carolina and Virginia. All the Iroquoian tribes of the Northeast inhabited a single ecological zone of deciduous forest with coniferous admixture, the evergreens tending to be more frequent toward the north. These tribes had much in common: much the same material culture, a similar economy, and social and political institutions that were closely parallel. Although many individual traits that are associated with the Iroquoian cultures of the Northeast were shared with adjacent non-Iroquoian peoples, the high degree of similarity among the northern Iroquoian cultures continues to justify Kroeber's (1939:91–92) assertion that there was a noteworthy correlation between ecological, linguistic, and cultural boundaries in this region.

---

[1] According to an alternative interpretation the name means "Speakers of a Common Language" (Jones 1909:419–420). In favor of the explanation cited above see Thwaites 1896–1901, Vol. XXXIII:237.

French and Hurons

The feelings that the French and Huron had about one another were influenced by their awareness of physical and cultural differences between them. Physical differences seem to have impressed the Huron more than they did the French. The French paid little attention to the physical characteristics of the Huron and considered them to be little different in appearance from themselves. The bronze complexion of the Huron was attributed mainly to their scanty dress and consequent exposure to the elements. Sagard noted that their hair was generally black, although some tended to be chestnut color. Like Mongoloids in general, the men had little facial hair and the Huron considered the beards of the Europeans to be grotesque and a sign of inferior intelligence. They also disapproved of curly hair, another instance where their taste proved embarrassing to the French.

Huron men are described as well-proportioned, robust, and on the average taller than Europeans. A large number of women had pleasing figures and facial features, and many of them were also tall. Cripples and other deformed individuals were rare, but were not entirely absent, as some overly enthusiastic accounts would have us believe. The French commented favorably on the intelligence of the Huron, which they felt was superior to that of peasants in their own country. Bressani praised the Hurons' ability to hear and the acuity of their vision, as well as their sense of direction and memory, the latter being best displayed in their ability to remember speeches. Bressani also noted that the Huron were indifferent to the odors of things that were not edible, and that they tended to open their lips in an awkward fashion. He attributed the latter to the lack of labial sounds in their language.

The Huron were trained from their youth to endure hardship and misfortune with patience and fortitude. In their dealings with one another they were gentle and considerate. Their frustrations and hostilities were largely vented on enemy tribes and on prisoners of war. This self-control may account for the often-repeated French comment that the Huron were cheerful and contented but "at all times a little taciturn." The Huron, for their part, viewed the European's talkativeness and their less inhibited expression of emotions with withering scorn.

The Europeans were offended by the Hurons' lack of cleanliness. Their houses were noisy, crowded, and smoky and abounded in fleas and lice, which the Jesuits believed were generated as a result of children urinating on the floor. The Huron did not wash their hands before eating, but if they were particularly dirty they wiped them on their hair or on a nearby dog. They also belched without any inhibition at their meals.

The Europeans frequently stated that the Huron were lazy. This appears to have been a false impression that arose because of the simple division of labor among the Huron. The latter was not conducive to the kind of routine labor to which the French were acccustomed.

Clothing

The Huron made their clothes out of well-prepared deerskin and beaver skins. These skins were obtained either from animals they killed or in trade with the Algonkians. In the hot weather a man wore only a breechclout made of deerskin and a pair of soft skin moccasins. Complete nudity, such as was common among the Neutral and some of the Algonkian tribes, was frowned on by the Huron. In addition, a man frequently wore a tobacco pouch that hung behind his back. This pouch served as a repository for any charms he might wish to carry with him. In the winter men also wore leggings that reached as high as the waist and sleeves that were held in place by a cord tied behind the back. Over the top of this a skin was worn as a cloak. Such clothing, crudely sewn together with leather strings, offered considerable protection against the cold. In spite of this, people are reported to have frozen to death every winter while traveling from one village to another. The fact that the Huron sought to obtain clothing, as well as skins, from the northern Algonkians suggests that these hunting peoples were able to manufacture clothing that was superior to that made by the Huron. The Huron women dressed the same as men did, except that in addition to a breechclout they wore a skirt extending from the waist part way to their knees. In the summer they left their bodies bare from the waist up.

Clothes were frequently decorated with red or brown paint and with various kinds of trimmings, including bands of porcupine quills dyed bright red. Some men wore feathers in their hair and made ruffs of down to fasten about their necks. Others wound long snake or eel skins round their foreheads, letting the ends hang down behind. Both men and women wore bracelets and necklaces made from shell beads. Strings of wampum were also hung from the ears and women carried bands of it slung seductively around their thighs. In addition, women wore large plaques encrusted with shell on their stomachs or hanging from their hair plaits. This finery was mostly in evidence at feasts and dances. At such times women might wear up to 12 pounds of shell beads.

The Huron were proud of their hair and spent much time looking after it. Women wore theirs in a single tress that hung down the back. This tress was tied with a leather thong or an eel skin. Men wore their hair in a variety of styles. Some arranged it in two large rolls above the ears, with the intervening area cut short; others shaved the sides of their head, leaving a roach down the center. Still others cut their hair in ridges or permitted one side to grow long while they cut the other. Men and women rubbed their hair with sunflower oil, and some colored it with various paints.

Men and women greased their bodies with oil and animal fat to protect them against the sun and cold. On special occasions, colors were added to make body paint. The principal colors were black and red, which were made from soot and from bloodroot and red ochre, respectively. The designs that were painted on a person appear to have included pictures of men and animals as well as stripes and other geometrical patterns. Some of these covered the whole body and were sufficiently well executed that at first glance the French mistook them for suits of clothing.

Some of the Huron, particularly women, appear to have been tattooed, but the latter practice was not as common among the Huron as it was among the Neutral and Tionontati.

Huronia

Although the Huron confederacy may have embraced more people than did any of the other Iroquoian ones, the Huron villages were concentrated in an area that measured no more than 35 miles east to west and 20 miles north to south (Fig. 1). The entire country could thus be traversed in a very leisurely fashion in three or four days. On the east the Huron settlements were bounded by Lake Simcoe, on the west by Nottawasaga Bay, the southernmost extension of Georgian Bay. The Huron country was separated from the region to the north by Matchedash Bay, a narrow inlet also opening onto Georgian Bay. There were a number of small lakes throughout Huronia, of which the three largest (Cranberry Lake, Orr Lake, and Bass Lake) were near its southern limits. Five short streams flow north through this region into Matchedash Bay. From west to east these rivers are called the Wye, Hog, Sturgeon, Coldwater, and North. Farther east, the waters of Lake Simcoe flow through Lake Couchiching and the Severn River to enter Matchedash Bay from the north.

Huronia is located on the northern limits of the rich farmland of southern Ontario. The region is underlaid by Trenton and Black River limestones and is covered with deep glacial tills. The soils that have developed on the tills and outwash are mainly sandy and well-drained, but because the material from which they were formed contained more Precambrian rock than is usual farther south, these soils differ from the normal gray-brown podsols of southern Ontario and have certain relationships with the brown podsolic soils to the north. Most of the soils in the more elevated regions are classified as Vasey sandy loams and are moderately stony, while the soils in the valleys are Tioga sandy loams, which are generally stone free. Both types of soil tend to dry out quickly and are poor in potassium, nitrogen, and phosphorus. From the Huron point of view, however, they had the great advantage of being easy to work. Intractable clay soils are found in the Nottawasaga drainage to the southwest of Huronia (Hoffman *et al.* 1962; Chapman and Putnam 1966:299–312).

Immediately north of Huronia, beginning at the east end of Matchedash Bay, the landscape changes. The deep deposits of till vanish and the hidden Paleozoic limestones of southern Ontario give way to the exposed metamorphic rock of the Canadian shield. This rock is covered only by scattered and often infertile patches of soil. Today this is a land of summer cottages and vacation resorts; three-hundred years ago it was the hunting grounds of the northern Algonkians.

The western section of Huronia is undulating, but nowhere does the land

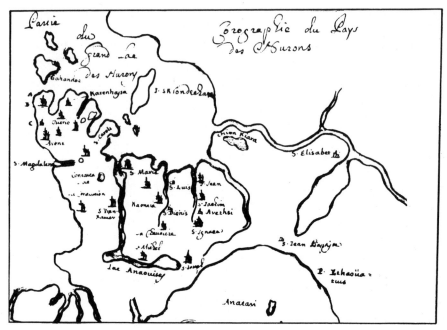

Fig. 1 *Above:* the Corographie du Pays des Hurons, *the best large-scale seven-teenth-century map of Huronia, shows the region between 1639 and 1648. Heiden-reich (1966:113) suggests that it may have been drawn by Jerome Lalemant. The names on the map are those assigned the Huron villages by the Jesuits.*
Below: a modern map showing the location of some of the major Huron settlements at the same period.

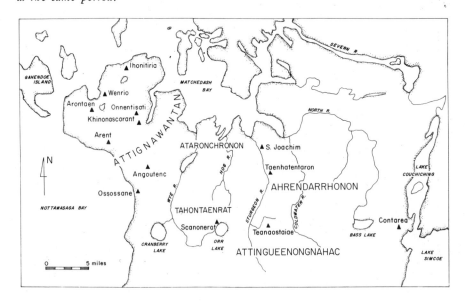

rise more than 500 feet above the waters of Lake Huron. In the north, especially around the heights overlooking Thunder Bay, the land rises quickly from the lake, but near the shores of Nottawasaga Bay there are vast areas covered with sand dunes and stunted vegetation. To the east there is a ridge of high ground between each of the rivers flowing north into Matchedash Bay. The northern ends of these ridges were scoured by the glacial lake Algonquin, which exposed large tracts of boulders. These areas are thoroughly unsuited for settlement. Nearer Lake Simcoe, the terrain becomes hilly and the land rises to over 1300 feet above sea level.

The original forests of Huronia consisted mostly of maple, beech, oak, and white pine. Various kinds of evergreens grew in the interior and in moister areas. Other trees found in Huronia include elm, birch, basswood, and ash. The clearing of these forests in the nineteenth century resulted in a considerable decline in the water table and the drying up of many creeks and springs. In the "dry hills" of Oro in the eastern part of Huronia the drop in the water table was as much as 30 feet. A similar drop in the water table following the Huron clearance of the forest in prehistoric times may explain why prehistoric, but not historic, sites are found in this region (Heidenreich 1967:23).

Before Huron settlement became extensive there must have been a considerable amount of wild life in Huronia, as there was throughout the rest of southern Ontario. The game animals were nonmigratory, deer, bear, and beaver being the most important. There were also large numbers of wild birds, including heron, geese, and turkeys. Even more important from the point of view of, subsistence, however, were the waters that surrounded Huronia and which even today teem with trout, pike, sturgeon, and other species of fish.

Southern Ontario has a temperate climate with four well-marked seasons. The climate of Huronia is not as favorable, however, as it is near Toronto or along the north shore of Lake Erie. The temperature of Huronia is lower than in these areas, but less so in summer than in winter. The daily mean temperature in Huronia in July is 65–70° F., in January, 15–20° F. The normal frost free period is 140–160 days, and the growing season is 180–200 days. This is long enough to assure a successful corn crop most years, but the margin of safety is less than it is in the Toronto area, where the growing season is 200 days. About 14.5 inches of rain fall between May and October and in general the rainfall is less in March and April than it is during the growing season. This has the advantage of permitting the soil to dry out quickly so that it can be cultivated early in the spring. The snowfall in Huronia is abundant: 90–110 inches per year as compared with 50–70 inches around Toronto. The average depth of the snow in winter is 20–30 inches.

Population

It is notoriously difficult to estimate aboriginal populations from historical data. Detailed statistical information is normally lacking, and the figures that have been recorded are often nothing more than fleeting impressions, more or less disguised. It is difficult enough for a person to judge the population of towns or the size of crowds in his own culture, and in an unfamiliar one the difficulties become multiplied.

The population that is usually quoted for the Huron prior to the epidemics that began to decimate them in 1636 is 30,000. This figure has been accepted as highly reliable because it is found in the writings of Champlain, Sagard, and the Jesuits. Its origin, however, deserves to be carefully scrutinized.

Champlain informs us that the Huron had "two thousand warriors, not including the common mass, which amounts to perhaps thirty thousand souls." This indicates a population of approximately 32,000. It is significant that Champlain does not claim this was his own estimate; rather he states that it was a figure quoted to him by the Huron. This raises two questions: (1) whether or not the Huron were able to estimate their total population accurately, and (2) whether or not Champlain understood them properly. It is strange that in a society in which all men, or at least all young men, were warriors the latter should have constituted less than seven percent of the total population. The main argument in favor of this figure is that Champlain, after visiting the different parts of Huronia, was willing to quote it.

Sagard's estimate of the Huron was 30,000–40,000. This suggests that he copied Champlain's figure, but believed it might be too low. Sagard did not visit all parts of Huronia, however, and there is reason to believe that in statistical matters he may have been given to exaggeration. Brebeuf continued to use the figure of 30,000 prior to his return to Huronia in 1634, apparently because it was the common estimate of the Huron population that was circulating among the French at that time. Since prior to 1640 the work of the Jesuits was mostly confined to the western part of Huronia, it is questionable whether they were in a better position than Sagard to judge the accuracy of this figure.

The most important statistical data concerning the size of the Huron population come from the Jesuit *Relation* of 1640. There Jerome Lalemant records that in 1639 the Jesuits visited all the Huron and Tionontati villages to gather information prior to the reorganization of the mission. As part of this survey the priests are said to have made a house-by-house census of the entire region. As a result, the Huron and Tionontati were found to have 32 villages, containing 700 cabins, 2000 hearths and 12,000 inhabitants. Since we are told elsewhere that two nuclear families normally shared the same hearth, these figures suggest that there were about 4000 families.

Even here, however, there are certain inconsistencies which suggest that these figures must be used with great caution. In particular, the suggestion that there were less than three hearths per cabin seems out of line with what is known about Huron longhouses from other textual sources and from the archaeological record. Moreover, there are historical reasons for suspecting that this survey was not as thorough as Father Lalemant's brief description implies. However, the low overall population and the unnaturally low figure of three persons in each family are not as unreasonable as they appear, the census having been taken after severe epidemics had swept the region. Similar epidemics killed large numbers of Indians in other parts of the New World (Dobyns 1966); hence, it would not be unusual if more than half the Hurons had perished prior to the end of 1639. Figures given elsewhere in the Jesuit relations suggest that in normal times a Huron family consisted of between five and eight people. Assuming that the figure of 2000 hearths provides an accurate indication of the number of families that was in the region prior to 1639, and estimating six people per family, we get a combined population of 24,000 for the Huron and the Tionontati prior to the epidemics. The relative proportion of the population that should be assigned to each of these two groups is unknown. The Jesuits write of 10,000 Huron after 1640, which suggests that the Tionontati numbered about 2000 at that time. Nevertheless, even if all but one or two of the Tionontati villages were hamlets, their nine villages, as compared with the Hurons' twenty or more, suggests that this figure is too low. Assuming that 9000 Huron survived the epidemics, one can suggest a pre-epidemic population for Huronia of about 18,000. Much more research remains to be done on the population of historic Huronia, and in future studies archaeological data will hopefully play an important role.

Settlement Patterns

It took considerable time for the French to discern the tribal structure of the Huron confederacy. Like the Iroquois, whose confederacy was made up of five tribes, the Mohawk, Oneida, Onondaga, Cayuga, and Seneca, the Huron consisted of a number of tribes, each having its own territory, councils, customs, and its own history. The main difference between the Huron and Iroquois confederacies lay in the distribution of their settlements. Among the Iroquois, the villages belonging to each tribe were separated from those of the next by stretches of forest that were used as hunting territory; among the Huron, the different tribes lived side by side and appear to have shared a common hunting territory. The greater proximity of the Huron tribes seems to have resulted in more intermarriage and a greater pooling of culture than was the case with the Iroquois. Linguistic variation was less marked among the Huron, and the French commentators were agreed that the Huron spoke a common language. Nevertheless, Sagard noted variations in the language spoken in different parts of the country, and there is clear evidence that the dialect of the Tahontaenrat was different from that of the Attignawantan (Thwaites 1896–1901, Vol. X:11). These differences in dialect appear to have developed at a time when the different tribes were geographically, as well as politically, separated from one another. Significant differences were also noted among the tribes in the religious sphere, the Attingueenongnahac, in particular, being renowned for the variety and complexity of their rituals. Even here, however, borrowing, which seems to have been leveling out cultural differences, was going on.

Champlain was unaware that the Huron belonged to different tribes. He referred to them collectively as the Attignawantan, which was the name of the westernmost of the Huron tribes. Later Sagard discerned three tribes: the Attignawantan, the Attingueenongnahac, who lived inland, and the Ahrendarrhonon (sometimes called the Contarearonon), who lived still farther east, near Lake

Simcoe. The Jesuits noted the existence of still another tribe, the Tahontaenrat, who occupied a single large village near the center of the country. According to the Jesuits, these four "nations" were the tribes that made up the Huron confederacy.

The Attignawantan was the largest and most powerful of these tribes. According to the Jesuits, about half the Huron population belonged to this tribe, which also appears to have held half the seats in the confederacy council. In 1640, the Attignawantan and the Attingueenongnahac claimed that they had formed the nucleus of the confederacy over 200 years before. On formal occasions the members of these tribes called each other "brother" and "sister" and appear to have been accorded special status as the founding members of the confederacy. The Ahrendarrhonon are reported to have joined the confederacy about 1590 and the Tahontaenrat about 1610. The Jesuits also mention another group, the Ataronchronon, who lived east of the Attignawantan near the shores of Matchedash Bay. The Ataronchronon inhabited a number of small villages, and Jones (1909: 447) surmises that they were not a tribe, but rather a miscellaneous collection of people who had settled near the protection of the Jesuit residence of Sainte-Marie. It is also possible that at least some of the villages administered by the Jesuit mission to the Ataronchronon may have been outlying villages of other tribes, such as the Attignawantan. The little that we know about the Ataronchronon suggests that they did not constitute a formal part of the Huron tribal system.

Various attempts have been made to determine the meaning of the names of the four Huron tribes. The French often referred to the Attignawantan as the "Nation of the Bear." It has been surmised that Ahrendarrhonon means the "People of the Rocks"; possibly a toponym since this tribe lived nearer than any of the others to the Canadian shield. The suggestions that Attingueenongnahac means "Cord People" and Tahontaenrat "Deer People" or "People of One Single White Lodge" are merely speculation.

Equally difficult are the problems of determining tribal boundaries and the tribal affiliations of some villages. These problems are particularly acute in the eastern part of Huronia, which was visited less frequently by the Europeans than was the western sector.

Champlain informs us that there were eighteen villages in Huronia, Sagard says twenty-five, and the Jesuits report twenty. In part, these differences may result from large villages dividing to form two or more new ones or from small villages joining together to form a single new one. Both of these occurrences are well attested to in the literature. The various figures may also reflect, however, a difference of opinion about the definition of a village. The largest villages in Huronia contained forty or more longhouses and probably had a population of 1500–2000 people in each.[2] There were about six of these large villages in Huronia, all of which appear to have been fortified. In addition, there were a number of smaller villages, many of which were unfortified. The inhabitants of these smaller villages fled to the larger settlements in times of danger and

---

[2] Champlain reports that in 1615 Cahiague, the principal village of the Ahrendarrhonon, was made up of two-hundred large houses, but this may well be an exaggeration.

attended council meetings and celebrations in the latter as well. Thus these small villages appear to have been satellites of the larger ones. Some hamlets appear to have consisted of only one or two cabins, and there may have been a difference of opinion in deciding whether or not to count these as villages.

According to the French, the Huron erected their principal villages on slightly elevated ground adjoining a good stream. Archaeological investigations have confirmed and elaborated these observations. Historic village sites tend to be located on natural eminences such as hills, old shorelines, or meander spurs. They are also located near good supplies of spring water and close to sandy well-drained soil which was favored for growing corn. The latter is found mostly on the sides and tops of hills rather than in the valley bottoms. Many of the village sites that have been mapped near the Sturgeon Valley are located on old lake terraces 200 feet or more above the present valley bottom, but near spots where springs flow from the sides of the hill (Heidenreich 1967:17–18). (Fig. 2.)

Villages were not built directly on the shores of Lake Huron because of soil conditions and to avoid the strong northwesterly winds that blow off the lake. Many of the Huron villages were located near the streams flowing north into Georgian Bay. Because these streams were short and rose within Huronia, they were useless to raiders from the south, but provided the Huron with excellent routes for traveling north onto Lake Huron.

The preferred location for a fortified village was on land surrounded by a slight natural depression. The oval palisades that protected these villages were not constructed like those of a European fort, but consisted of wooden poles 15 feet or more high and often only a few inches in diameter. These poles were pointed at the base and were twisted into the ground a few inches apart. Usually there were three rows of stakes, one inside the other. These rows were woven together with smaller branches and reinforced in between with large pieces of bark. The base of the palisade was further strengthened by piling earth against it or by fastening tree trunks lengthwise in front of it. Watchtowers and galleries were constructed on the inside of the wall and were reached by ladders made of notched logs. If an attack was expected, the galleries were stocked with rocks to hurl at the enemy and water to put out fires. Usually a village had only one entrance. The two ends of the palisade were made to overlap in such a way that it was necessary for a person to turn at a right angle upon entering or leaving the village. The entrance passage was protected by bars rather than by a gate.

In 1636 the Attignawantan occupied fourteen villages. Most of these were small and unfortified. The principal town was the walled village of Ossossane, located near the southern border of Huronia. This town had approximately eight small villages dependent on it. Farther north, in the Penetanguishene Peninsula, were five more villages, which appear to have had the fortified village of Angoutenc as their nucleus. At the time of Sagard's visit, Khinonascarant was the main town in the north, but between 1623 and 1637 it split into three hamlets.

The villages of the three eastern tribes appear to have been fewer in number but larger than those of the Attignawantan. Most of them were walled villages. The Tahontaenrat occupied a single large village, called Scanonerat. Unfortunately, it is not clear how many villages belonged to the other two tribes

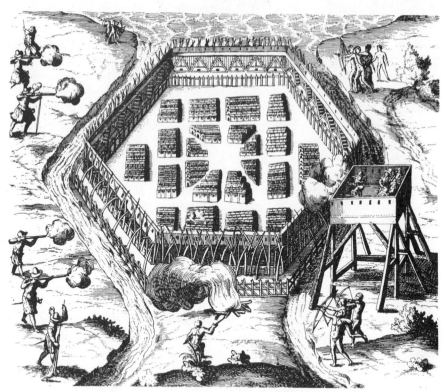

Fig. 2 No contemporary drawing of a Huron village has been preserved. This picture of an Iroquois village under attack by Champlain and his Huron allies in 1615 provides an idea of what a large Iroquoian village looked like to the French. Archaeological evidence indicates that both the "open square" and "streets" are highly idealized.

or which villages these were. The Jesuit *Relations* of 1636 speak of a confederacy council attended by the Attignawantan and two other tribes that had four villages each. If the Tahontaenrat is here being counted as part of the Attingueenongnahac or Ahrendarrhonon, it is likely that the two latter tribes had seven villages between them.

One of the large Ahrendarrhonon villages was Contarea. It was located near Lake Couchiching and appears to be the same village that the French called Saint Jean Baptiste (Heidenreich 1966:123–124). Another Ahrendarrhonon village, described as the "chief bulwark of the country," was destroyed by the Iroquois in 1642. Still a third is, possibly, the one that was known to the French by the name of Saint Joachim. This village was located just east of the Sturgeon River. The important village of Taenhatentaron appears to have been either Ahrendar-rhonon or Attingueenongnahac. It was located in the Sturgeon Valley not far south of Saint Joachim. Still farther south was Teanaostaiae. At the time of the Jesuit mission this village was said to be the largest in Huronia. It was the principal village of the Attingueenongnahac and was the southernmost village in

Huronia along the trail that led south to the Neutral country. West of it was Ekhiondastsaan, apparently also a village of the Attingueenongnahac.

Because so many of the villages of the Attignawantan were small ones, it is possible that this tribe contained less than half of the total population of the confederacy, even though it was the largest tribe. From the point of view of Huron subsistence activities, small villages probably had a number of advantages over large ones. Because fewer fields were required, a village could remain in the same place longer without exhausting all the land and firewood within easy reach; hence villages had to be moved less often. If farming had been their only concern, the northern Iroquoians might have preferred to live in small villages.

One of the advantages of larger villages must have been that life in them was more exciting. In historic times such villages clearly were the focus of ritual activity. More important, however, these villages could be defended more easily than small, scattered ones. Being protected from Iroquois attack on account of their location, the Attignawantan had less need of large, fortified villages than had the other Huron tribes. It is significant that Ossossane, their largest village, was located on the exposed southern border of Attignawantan territory. It is also significant that when the Huron felt themselves threatened by an Iroquois attack in 1635, the five northern Attignawantan villages discussed building a single fortified village, a plan that was abandoned when the danger diminished. The three eastern tribes were much more exposed to Iroquois raiding parties, so much so that in the border villages women frequently had to be guarded while they worked in the fields. This is probably the reason why the members of these tribes grouped themselves together in a small number of large, well-fortified settlements.[3]

Neighboring Tribes

The Iroquoian population of the Northeast tended to live in populous but widely separated clusters; hence the dense settlement in Huronia was not typical of most of southern Ontario. Indeed, in spite of the better climate along the north shore of Lake Ontario, the region south of the Canadian shield between Toronto and Kingston seems to have been completely uninhabited. This triangle was the main hunting territory of the Huron.

West of Huronia near the rugged part of the Niagara escarpment known as the Blue Mountain, lived the Tionontati, also referred to as the Petun or Tobacco nation. Although far less numerous than the Huron, the two groups spoke the same language and had similar customs. The Tionontati lived in nine

---

[3] Satisfying as this picture is, a caution must be noted. The Jesuits spent the early years of their stay in Huronia among the Attignawantan and did not work extensively with the other three tribes until after 1640. By this time the struggle over the fur trade was reaching a climax. Had they arrived in the outlying areas at a slightly earlier period, when conditions were more peaceful, they might have found more small dispersed villages and a general settlement pattern resembling that of the Attignawantan. Some support for this conclusion appears to be found in the moderately high number of historic sites that has been located in the eastern part of Huronia.

villages, only one or two of which seem to have been of any size. Ehwae, their principal villege, was burned by a hostile tribe, perhaps the Assistaronon, in 1640.

Farther south, from the Grand River Valley, north of Lake Erie, eastward across the Niagara River lived another Iroquoian confederacy that was known to the French as the Neutral nation and to the Huron as the Attiwandaron. The latter was a term that the Huron and Neutral applied to each other and it meant "peoples who speak a slightly different language." The implication that the Neutral language was less different from Huron than were the languages of the Iroquois is in harmony with the archaeological record, which suggests that the culture of these two groups did not begin to diverge before A.D. 1400 (the ethnic and linguistic differentiation may, of course, have begun earlier).

The Neutral confederacy was made up of several tribes, three or four of which are recorded on early maps. Prior to 1639 the Wenro, another Iroquoian people who lived near the Seneca in New York State, appear to have been associated with the Neutral confederacy. At that time, the growing hostility of the Seneca is said to have forced at least some of the Wenro to settle among the Huron.

The Neutral differed from the Huron in a number of ways. They kept the bodies of their dead in their dwellings for long periods of time, and after the flesh had decayed they returned the bones to their houses, where they kept them until the Feast of the Dead was celebrated. Their ossuaries were smaller and constructed differently from those of the Huron. Like the Tionontati, the Neutral were fond of tattooing their bodies.

Wild fruits and nuts were plentiful in the Neutral country, which was warmer than Huronia. Animals were also exceedingly abundant, and the Neutral are described as being excellent hunters. Although their population appears to have been smaller than that of the Huron, they are said to have occupied forty villages and hamlets. This suggests that most of their villages were small ones, and this, combined with the fact that these villages were more broadly dispersed than those of the Huron, may reflect a greater dependence on hunting (Trigger 1963a).

The Neutral were so called because they refused to become involved in the long-standing feud between the Huron and the Iroquois. Both of the latter were free to visit their villages and were forced to respect the peace there. The Neutral waged war against the Assistaronon or Fire Nation, an Algonkian people, uncertainly identified as the Mascouten. The Assistaronon were also the enemies of the Tionontati and they appear to have commanded, and perhaps even inhabited, the eastern shore of Lake Huron south of the Bruce Peninsula, although their main tribal territory seems to have been in Michigan. As yet, no archaeological finds have helped to shed light on their activities in Ontario.

Most of the interior of southwestern Ontario was uninhabited and was used as hunting territory by the Neutral and Petun. A number of small Algonkian-speaking tribes lived along the southern shores of Georgian Bay, while still others lived in the Bruce Peninsula. The best known of these groups were the Cheveux Releves, who lived west of the Tionontati, probably in the vicinity of the Beaver Valley. The Cheveux Releves grew corn, but also traveled extensively. In 1615

Champlain encountered three hundred of them drying blueberries near the northeast corner of Georgian Bay. In later years these people were known as the Ottawa.

The Huron were familiar with a number of tribes who lived south of the Great Lakes; all of them Iroquoian-speaking. Five of these tribes, the Mohawk, Oneida, Onondaga, Cayuga, and Seneca, were joined together to form a confederacy similar to that of the Huron. The French called these tribes the Iroquois, a term of obscure origin. Each of these tribes occupied one to three major villages, as well as a number of small hamlets. Most of the larger Iroquois villages were fortified. Indeed, Champlain described the fortifications of the village he attacked in 1615 as being superior to those built by the Huron. Villages belonging to the same tribe were located close to one another, but since each tribe built its settlements near the center of its hunting territory, villages belonging to different tribes were between 10 and 40 miles apart. Five clusters of Iroquois settlement were stretched across upper New York State between the Mohawk Valley and the Niagara frontier.

No reliable information is available concerning the population of the Iroquois confederacy in the first half of the seventeenth century. The aboriginal population is often quoted as being about 12,000, or half that of the Huron. Especially when we consider the small size of many Attignawantan villages, the ten or so large communities that the Iroquois are recorded as occupying do not suggest a population notably less than that of the Huron. The Iroquois, like the Huron, were stricken by serious epidemics in the late 1630s and early 1640s, and it is not impossible that prior to this time the population of both confederacies was about 18,000–20,000. As a result of the epidemics, both confederacies appear to have lost over half their population. Further losses from war and disease may explain the failure of the Iroquois to increase in spite of the many captives they incorporated into their society after 1640.

The Iroquois were the only tribes with whom the Huron were consistently at war during the historic period. According to the Huron, the two confederacies had been fighting for over fifty years. The nearest and most feared of the Iroquois tribes were the Seneca.

Another Iroquoian group, known as the Erie or Cat nation, lived near the southeast corner of Lake Erie. Like their neighbors, the Erie were horticulturalists inhabiting a number of sedentary villages. The most southerly Iroquoian tribe with whom the Huron were in contact was the Andastes or Susquehannock. This tribe lived in the Susquehanna Valley, almost 400 miles south of Huronia. Like the Huron, the Susquehannock were at war with the Iroquois; hence the two groups recognized each other as allies. Although the Iroquois tried to prevent contact between the Huron and the Susquehannock, diplomatic missions and warriors seeking adventure secretly made their way through the intervening Iroquois territory to get from one group to the other. In 1647 a number of Susquehannock were reported to be living in Huronia.

The country north of Huronia was entirely occupied by Algonkian-speaking peoples who subsisted mainly by hunting and fishing. Some of the tribes that lived near Lake Nipissing or in the Ottawa Valley planted corn, but only in small amounts and as a supplement to their diet. Because of their subsistence pattern, the northern hunters were fewer in number, more dispersed, and less sedentary than were the agricultural tribes to the south, whether the latter were Algonkian or Iroquoian speaking.

All of the northern tribes appear to have had good relations with the Huron, and many obtained supplies of corn from them. The Huron were thoroughly familiar with the bands that inhabited the shores of Georgian Bay, as well as with the Nipissing, an important group that had its headquarters near Lake Nipissing and traveled as far north as James Bay each summer, and with the various Algonkian bands that inhabited the Ottawa Valley. Even in the sixteenth century the Huron appear to have been in contact with tribes that lived in the interior of Quebec, perhaps as far east as Tadoussac. The Huron also visited the Upper Great Lakes and traded with such tribes as the Winnebago, who lived on the western shore of Lake Michigan.

Travel

The tribes we have been mentioning are those that the Huron knew well and with whom they interacted. The extent of these contacts should dispel any notion that the agricultural peoples of the Northeast were isolated or provincial at this time. Even though their contacts with the south were limited, the Huron knew more about what the Dutch and English settlers were doing along the eastern seaboard of America than did the French who were living in Quebec.

The Huron normally traveled on foot throughout Huronia and when they visited the other tribes of southwestern Ontario. A network of trails joined the various Huron villages together, the main trails following the ridges where the forest was less thick. Beyond Huronia an important trail ran from Ossossane westward toward the Tionontati country, while another went south from Teanaostaiae, then turned west toward Kandoucho, the nearest Neutral village. The Huron usually carried with them only their bowl, spoon, and a sleeping mat, since food and shelter were provided for them in the various towns they visited. In winter, snowshoes were used to travel long distances and heavy loads were carried on sledges.

When trading in the north, visiting their hunting grounds, or making their way across Lake Ontario to attack the Iroquois, the Huron traveled by canoe. Among the nomadic tribes to the north entire families traveled by canoe, but among the Huron this form of travel seems to have been largely restricted to men. Like the northern Algonkians, the Huron covered their canoes with birchbark. These canoes were superior to those of the Iroquois and Neutral, which had to be made of elm or hickory bark since the canoe birch did not grow in their tribal territories. Although light and therefore easy to carry around portages, the Huron canoes were fragile and tended to leak. Because of this, the Huron usually stayed within sight of land. The main water route to the north was along the island-studded east shore of Georgian Bay, at the north end of which the Huron could turn either eastward through Lake Nipissing or west along the north shore of Lake Huron toward Lakes Superior and Michigan. Although fish and game were caught along the way, the Huron traveler carried a supply of cornmeal with him, as well as a clay pot that at various times was used to bail out the canoe, cook meals, and to urinate in so as not to upset the canoe. Each evening the boat was landed on the shore and some men erected a rough birchbark shelter while others collected firewood and cooked the evening meal. Another meal was eaten in the morning before breaking camp. During the day, the Huron did not stop to eat, although they frequently smoked to deaden their hunger. If a man planned to return along the same route, corn wrapped in birchbark bags was deposited in caches at two-day intervals for the return journey. Travelers also erected signs along the route, painted on slabs of bark and recording the village from which they came as well as the number of men who were in the group.

Prehistory

The French writers tell us little about the historical lore of the Huron, although this was one of the subjects they discussed with them. We have already mentioned that the Huron told Jerome Lalemant that the Attignawantan and Attingueenongnahac had founded the confederacy over two-hundred years before and that the Ahrendarrhonon had joined it about 1590 and the Tahontaenrat about 1610. If this story is correct, the nucleus of the Huron confederacy may predate the formation of the Iroquois league. For further information we must turn to the archaeological record.

Until recently, because of their similarities in language and culture, it was believed that the northern Iroquoians had arrived in the Lower Great Lakes region a few centuries prior to the historic period and that they had brought with them a culture that had its origins in the southeast. It was argued that they had arrived in the Northeast as a single people, but had gradually drifted apart to form the tribes that existed in the seventeenth century.

This theory is no longer supported by archaeological and linguistic evidence. It is clear that, rather than being intrusive, the northern Iroquoian cultures developed out of the indigenous woodland cultures of an earlier period. Before the developmental relationship between the Iroquoian cultures and these earlier ones was recognized, it was believed that the latter had been produced by Algonkian-speaking groups which the Iroquoians had driven from the region. It is also clear from linguistic evidence that the northern Iroquoians were already split into ethnic divisions roughly corresponding to certain of the historic tribes long before "Iroquoian culture" had developed. Glottochronological studies[4] indicate that the Seneca, Cayuga, and Oneida languages were already separate by A.D. 800 at the latest, and the split between the Iroquois languages and Huron appears to have

---

[4] Glottochronology is the study of types and rates of change in language over time, using rates of change in the basic vocabulary to estimate the time separating two stages of a single language or the time since two related languages have diverged from a common form.

occurred appreciably earlier (Lounsbury 1961:12). The evolution of the historic Iroquoian cultures can thus be viewed as a process of parallel development involving a number of distinct peoples speaking related languages.

Prior to A.D. 1000 the peoples of the Northeast appear to have subsisted mainly by hunting and fishing. Bands gathered together in large summer camps and dispersed in the winter to family hunting territories. After that time, corn agriculture became more important and small palisaded villages began to appear. At first, these villages were thinly scattered over wide areas and cultural contact between different tribes was probably easier than it was in later times. The fact that neighboring Iroquoian-speaking groups were able to communicate with each other more easily than with Algonkian-speakers may account for the many cultural features that came to be shared by the different Iroquoian tribes. Although nearby Algonkian groups participated in the development of various features of "Iroquoian culture," they did so to a lesser degree. The Algonkians to the north of Huronia were, of course, excluded from participating in many of the basic features of Iroquoian culture by environmental factors.

By A.D. 1300 most of southern Ontario west of Kingston was occupied by a single, homogeneous culture. The earlier and later phases of this culture have been termed by archaeologists Uren and Middleport, respectively. At this time the population appears to have been living in small villages, thinly scattered over much of the region. Cooked human bones begin to appear in the village middens at this time suggesting warfare, even if raids were still limited to neighboring villages. Warfare in turn may have promoted defensive alliances and encouraged the formation of larger villages, the clustering together of villages belonging to the same tribe, and, finally, the formation of confederacies.

As a result of these developments, the population of southern Ontario became concentrated in certain well-defined areas and the cultural uniformity of the region began to break down. By A.D. 1400, a culture ancestral to that of the historic Neutral and Erie can be distinguished north and east of Lake Erie, while a proto-Huron culture is found distributed in a triangle between Georgian Bay, Toronto, and Kingston. A continuation of the latter culture westward along the south shore of Georgian Bay is probably associated with the culturally similar Tionontati.

Within the proto-Huron culture a number of local clusterings of settlement can be distinguished. The material culture of the villages in north Simcoe County (historic Huronia) was different from that found in the Toronto area, and, although it has not been studied in detail, the culture of groups that lived farther east in the Trent Valley seems to have been slightly different again. It is tempting to associate these divisions of proto-Huron culture with the various tribes that later made up the Huron confederacy. Wright (1966:78–80) has suggested that the Attignawantan and Attingueenongnahac may have been the original groups resident in the north part of Simcoe County, and the Jesuits' apparent statement that these tribes could point out the sites of former villages as far back as two-hundred years seems to support this idea. If this is so, the principal groups living to the south and east were probably the Ahrendarrhonon and Tahontaenrat. However, it is not impossible that the Jesuits were recording what they had learned from the Attignawantan alone and that the statement about village sites applies only to them. The alliance between this tribe and the Attingueenongnahac may have been concluded a considerable time before the two groups actually settled side by side. Moreover, it is noteworthy that the groups who lived in the Toronto area appear to have moved into Huronia by 1550, a half century before the Ahrendarrhonon are stated to have arrived there. This suggests that the Attignawantan may have originally inhabited Huronia, while the Attingueenongnahac lived to the south and the Ahrendarrhonon and Tahontaenrat to the southeast. This reconstruction, although very tentative in view of our present knowledge of Ontario prehistory, would account for the substantial numbers of prehistoric sites that are known to exist north of Lake Ontario.

It thus appears that in the past each of the Huron tribes was geographically separate from the others, and had its own hunting territory. The settlement pattern of the Hurons around 1550 probably resembled that of the Iroquois a hundred years later. Sometime in the late sixteenth century, however, there was a shift in Huron settlement that was unparalleled among the Iroquois. All the tribes living north of Lake Ontario moved into the northern part of Simcoe County, where they settled next to one another. The land they had formerly occupied became the joint hunting territory of the Huron confederacy as a whole.

The movement of two or three additional tribes into the area between Lake Simcoe and Georgian Bay must have affected the distribution of the indigenous communities, and continuing need for adjustments may explain why in historic times there is no clear-cut relationship between the areas occupied by the various tribes and natural geographic features. It is noteworthy that the highest density of prehistoric villages within Huronia is in the hilly country near Lake Simcoe (Heidenreich 1967:23). This may have been the main area of settlement in prehistoric times, and it may have been from there that the Attignawantan moved into the western part of Huronia as later arrivals moved in from the south and east.

The questions that remain to be settled are: (1) why did the Huron choose to settle near the shores of Georgian Bay, and (2) why did the Huron tribes locate their villages side by side while the tribes of the Iroquois confederacy chose to keep theirs apart from one another?

The traditional explanation has been that the Huron were forced to flee to Huronia because of the attacks of the Iroquois. There, with their backs to Georgian Bay, they were imagined to be making a last stand against the enemy at the time when they began trading with the French. The Huron were obviously concerned about Iroquois raids and carefully fortified the villages that were most exposed to attack; this, however, was a common practice of all the Iroquoian tribes. More specific support for this hypothesis has been found in Champlain's surmise that the Trent Valley, east of Huronia, was abandoned because of fear of the Iroquois. Moreover, in 1639 the Wenro, a small tribe from New York State who were being attacked by the Iroquois, fled to Huronia.

It may be that fear of the Iroquois induced certain small tribes to move north in order to escape Iroquois attack. This does not explain, however, why a substantial number of Huron appear to have lived in Huronia from the earliest stages in the development of Iroquoian culture. The theory also seems to be based on incorrect assessment of the military capabilities of the Huron in relation to the Iroquois. It is clear that prior to the time when the Iroquois acquired more guns than the Huron were able to obtain, the latter were never at the Iroquois' mercy. Year after year, Huron raiding parties entered the Iroquois country and returned with prisoners to be tortured to death. Moreover, the Iroquois tribes were at war not only with the Huron but also with the Susquehannock to the south and various Algonkian tribes to the east and northeast. In spite of this, the Iroquois were not driven to settle near one another, and rare was the time when all five tribes fought against a common enemy. While the outbreak of war with the Iroquois may explain why tribes such as the Ahrendarrhonon and Tahontaenrat wished to be on good terms with the other Huron tribes, it does not provide a reason for them to have settled in Huronia. Instead, some quite different reasons deserve serious consideration.

From an Iroquoian point of view, Huronia had many natural advantages. Although the region was colder than the land just north of Lakes Erie and Ontario, there was a vast amount of sandy soil there. This was the sort of soil that the Iroquoians needed because it was easy to work. Similar land was available elsewhere, but its particular abundance in Huronia may explain why some groups had lived there from the start. Huronia had other unique advantages. It was surrounded on three sides by lakes and rivers that abounded in fish and in places where fish could be caught easily. This was important, since fish constituted the main source of protein in the Huron diet.

Even more important, Huronia was located on the very edge of the Canadian shield and at the south end of the only along-shore canoe trail leading to the north. In the latter region lived the Algonkian hunters, who had a surplus of furs and dried fish and meat to trade with the Huron, as well as exotic items such as pieces of copper and buffalo skins, which they obtained in trade at Sault Saint Marie and beyond. These tribes were anxious to obtain stores of corn to hold them over the winter, as well as tobacco and other products from the south. There is evidence of contacts between Huronia and the north beginning in early times, and it would appear that over the years a symbiotic relationship developed between the inhabitants of these two regions. This interdependence goes a long way toward explaining why the Huron chose to settle in the southeast corner of Georgian Bay, as well as the friendly relations that prevailed between the Huron and the northern Algonkians (Trigger 1962), a friendship that earlier writers saw as unnatural and transgressing every bond of race and language. The objection that a nomadic people would have been more likely to move toward an agricultural one than the reverse (Heidenreich 1967:16) completely ignores the unique location of Huronia on the edge of the Canadian shield and at the head of an important water route to the north.

In this connection it is worth noting that while the main clusters of sites containing European trade goods occur within the area where Champlain and Sagard reported the Huron were living, a smaller number are found to the south and east of this region. It is possible that some of these sites were hunting camps or resting places used in the historic period. It is also possible, however, that

European trade goods were reaching Huronia for a considerable period prior to Champlain's visit; if so, these sites appear to indicate that the settlement pattern was less concentrated in late prehistoric times than it was immediately afterward. It is possible that the distribution of Huron settlements in historic times, when villages were restricted to the Penetanguishene Peninsula and along the creeks flowing into Georgian Bay, was the result of an intensification of trade with the north that came about with the development of the fur trade. If so, this final concentration of population was the culmination of a process that had begun long before the arrival of the Europeans.

3

The Huron Economy

A S IN MOST CLASSLESS SOCIETIES, the principal distinction that was made in Huron social structure was sex difference. Among the Huron, this fundamental distinction was emphasized to the degree that everyday relations between men and women appear to have generated feelings of uneasiness and were characterized by a considerable amount of formality and avoidance. (Quain 1937:276). Huron men were anxious to assert their masculinity and to this end spent much of their time pursuing dangerous activities outside the community. Even in the villages, life was organized in such a way that men and women spent much of every day apart from one another. The Huron did not approve of public displays of intimacy between' the sexes, and a man was ashamed to be seen arguing with a woman. Nowhere, however, is the distinction between the sexes more evident than in the division of labor, particular tasks being considered appropriate to each sex. Even young boys refused to perform women's tasks, and men were subjected to public ridicule if necessity compelled them to do so in the presence of a woman.

Iroquoian women are generally credited with producing most of the food that was eaten, and it is often suggested that the matrilineal tendencies in Iroquoian society are a reflection of this. A popular picture of Huron life shows the women toiling in their cornfields while the men entertain themselves hunting, fishing, and fighting or give themselves up to festivities and relaxation. Champlain and Sagard are largely responsible for this picture, but their opinions about how the Huron earned a living were much influenced by their understanding of rural life in France. The result, as we shall see, was to do Huron men an injustice.

Horticulture

There is no question that in historic times the Huron subsistence pattern was predominantly based on horticulture. Crop yields accounted for perhaps three-quarters of all the food that was eaten. Maize was the most important crop, constituting the staple food of the Huron. There is also no doubt that the planting, care, and harvesting of food crops were women's tasks. Tobacco was grown by the men, but only in small patches near their longhouses.[1]

A striking feature of Huron food production, and of food production in the eastern woodlands generally, is the limited variety of plants that was cultivated. Indian corn, beans, and squash were the three plants that were grown to be eaten. Sunflowers were planted for their seed, from which oil was extracted which the Huron used to garnish food and to rub on their bodies. Some tobacco was cultivated as well, although this plant grew better among the Tionontati and the Neutral, because the climate in their region was milder. All these plants were of southern origin, the sunflower being indigenous to the eastern United States, the rest to Mesoamerica. Maize and tobacco appear to have been present in Ontario prior to A.D. 1000, but the sunflower did not arrive until 1300, and beans and squash not before 1400 (Wright 1966:98). Considering the climate of Huronia and its location on the extreme northern limits of New World agriculture, it is not surprising that only a few of the most important and adaptable of the Mesoamerican cultigens made their way this far north.

The Huron women worked the soil with small wooden spades. As a result, agriculture was restricted to the light sandy terrain of the sort that was common in Huronia. Because these soils dry out easily, there was much anxiety about drought. Late spring frosts sometimes killed the seedlings and made it necessary to resow the fields, and in the summer the crops were threatened by insects. Champlain states that because of their fear of famine the Huron planted enough corn every spring to last them several years. Later reports of famine following crop failures suggest, however, that most of this surplus production was used for trade. Crop failures often involved only a few villages, in which case corn was obtained from other parts of the country. If the crop failure was more widespread, the Huron sought to obtain corn from the Neutral and Tionontati and relied more on hunting and collecting.

The most arduous agricultural task, although it is the one to which the French paid the least attention, was that of clearing land. This was men's work. Armed with stone axes, the men cut down the smaller trees, then girdled the larger ones and stripped off their branches. These branches were burned at the base of the larger trees to kill them. Crops were then planted between the stumps. The latter were only removed when they became rotten and could be broken up easily. This was slow work, and prior to the acquisition of iron axes, the clearing of new fields had to begin several years before they were needed. It was also an unremitting task, particularly since Huron agricultural practices forced them to relocate their villages every ten to twenty years. This was necessary because without the addition of new organic material continuous use quickly depleted the fertility of the soil, and the clearance of new fields around a village

---

[1] Pierre Boucher (1664) says that among the Huron "c'est eux [les hommes] qui font les champs de tabac." The Jesuit *Relations* report that a Huron named Chihwatenha, a native of Ossossane, had a small plot of tobacco near his cabin (Thwaites 1896–1901, Vol. XV:79).

eventually exhausted nearby supplies of wood that were suitable for fires and building houses. Unless threatened with extermination, the Iroquoians rarely moved their villages more than a few miles at a time. This allowed the men to clear fields in the new location prior to the actual move. When a longer move was necessary, the refugees would try to settle near an existing village where they might obtain provisions and borrow fields where they could grow crops to hold them over for the first few years. A move into virgin territory would spell disaster for any sizable group.

It is uncertain how much land in Huronia was under cultivation at any one time. Assuming the population to have been about 30,000, Robert Popham (1950) has estimated that 390,000 bushels of corn were needed each year, and 23,300 acres were required to grow this much. However, on the basis of his observation of subsistence patterns on Iroquois reservations in New York State, Fenton (personal communication) is inclined to believe that 7000 acres would have been enough to support a population of 20,000. In spite of extensive cornfields and abandoned clearings not yet grown over with new trees, there were still extensive tracts of forest within the heart of Huronia. Moreover, there is no evidence that particular sites were being reinhabited at regular intervals. Even in Huronia, the pressure on land does not appear to have been great enough to induce particular communities to occupy a number of specified sites in rotation.

Any man could clear as much land as he wished, and this land remained in the possession of his family members as long as they wished to cultivate it. Once abandoned, however, a field could be planted by anyone who wished to do so. It is unclear to what degree each woman regarded the corn, beans, and squash she produced as her own property or whether or not the women living in a single longhouse considered all the food they produced to be their common possession. It is significant, however, that the large vats or casks that were used to store corn were located in the porch or in some corner of the longhouse, not in the divisions belonging to individual families. The reciprocity and sharing among the kinsmen that inhabited a single longhouse must have encouraged the *de facto* pooling of their resources.

In the spring, the Huron women carefully cleaned their fields and prepared their corn for planting by sorting the kernels and soaking them in water for several days. Nine or ten kernels were then planted in "holes" or "pits" a few feet apart, which Sagard informs us were used year after year. It appears that these "holes" were in fact cornhills: low hillocks of soft earth that the women scraped together and into which they shoved their seed. The remains of fields dotted with these cornhills, each several feet in diameter, were still visible when Huronia was resettled during the last century. It is unclear whether or not, like some other tribes, the Huron planted their corn, beans, and squash in the same fields. To avoid the danger of late frosts the women placed their squash seeds in bark trays filled with powdered wood, which they kept near the fires in their longhouses. After the seeds had sprouted, the young plants were transferred to the fields.

In the parts of the country that were sheltered from enemy raiders, the women often left the villages during the summer and went with their children to live in cabins near their fields. During the summer the women took great care to keep their fields clean of weeds, while the children chased away birds and animals. The corn, which belonged to the Northern Flint variety, grew over 6 feet high, matured in three or four months, and bore two or three ears, each yielding 100 kernels or more. When the corn was harvested, the leaves were turned up and the cobs tied in bundles that were hung from poles under the roofs of the houses. When the kernels were dry and fit for storage, the women shelled and cleaned them, then stored them in large vats. Young corn was preserved by picking the cobs before they were ripe and roasting them. Sliced squash remained edible for up to five months.

Because the Huron feared drought and frost, they sought supernatural protection against such disasters. Certain shamans claimed to be able to control the weather. Some would predict frost, suggesting at the same time that it could be prevented if the Huron burned a little tobacco each day in their fields to honor the sky. In times of drought others would promise to produce rain in return for public gifts. Under their direction feasts were given to end the drought. If these rituals were not successful, the shaman sought to protect his reputation by attributing his failure to sorcery or other malign influences. If he had a series of failures, the people generally lost faith in him.

Collecting

In addition to caring for the crops, the women gathered a wide variety of wild plants, which served to add flavor to an otherwise bland diet. Berries of many kinds were collected, and some were dried for winter use, as treats for the sick, to flavor corn soup, or to put into small cakes that were baked in ashes. Acorns, walnuts, and grapes were also commonly eaten. The Jerusalem artichoke (*Helianthus tuberosus*), a wild relative of the sunflower, was rare in Huronia, but its tubers were eaten, either raw or cooked, as was *sondhratates* (either ground nuts, *Apios americana*, or cow parsnip, *Heracleum lanatum*). Ripe chives were baked in ashes.

Several plants required special treatment before being eaten. Plums were bitter prior to being touched by the frost unless they were buried in the ground before being eaten. Acorns were boiled several times to take away the bitter taste. In times of crop failure, wild plants became an important item in the Huron diet. At such times, in addition to the wild plants that were normally eaten the Huron ate various kinds of tree bark, mosses, and lichen.

The women also gathered all the wood that was needed for cooking and heating the houses. Dry wood was preferred because it produced less smoke, and women often went considerable distances to obtain it. They did not collect twigs or wood from the trunks of large trees, which were left to rot because the Huron did not have the tools to cut them up. The best wood was available after the winter storms had knocked the dead limbs from the trees. During two days in March or April the women from each village helped one another to collect all the wood that was needed for the following year. This wood was tied in fagots, which the women carried back to the village on a tumpline. If a girl married at a time of year when wood was difficult to obtain, the women of the village gave her some of their own as a present. The firewood was stored in the porches and living quarters of the longhouse.

Another communal activity was the gathering of Indian hemp (*Apocynum cannabinum*), a plant that grew in marshy and humid places and from which rope was made. If there was danger of enemy attack, some warriors would accompany the women and sometimes might help them gather the hemp. Rope was also made from shredded and boiled basswood bark.

Hunting and Fishing

The importance of fishing for the subsistence economy of the Huron has been greatly underrated. Moreover, since fishing was mainly a male activity, the role of men in the Huron economy has been simultaneously underestimated. Much fishing was done with a wooden spear to which a barbed head made of bone was attached. Numerous examples of these "harpoon heads" have been found in archaeological sites. It appears that even more fishing was done with nets made out of Indian hemp rope. Net fishing was done on the open water and at the openings in weirs. The most celebrated and important set of weirs was those built at the narrows between Lakes Simcoe and Couchiching. Traces of what appear to be the poles that made up these weirs were noted and described earlier in the present century. The Huron also fished with hook and line, the hook being made of wood with a bone bar attached, but since the lines were weak, this was not a particularly effective method.

Various kinds of fish were caught in different places and at different seasons of the year. The most important fishing expeditions were those made in the autumn to the many islands in Georgian Bay to catch the whitefish (in Huron, *assihendo*) that fed there at that time. These trips often lasted a month or more. The fishermen, made up of groups each with its own leader, selected a particular island as their base of operations and proceeded to erect a bark house on the island. They built these in the Algonkian fashion: a typical cabin containing two fireplaces and sheltering four parties, one in each corner. Each evening, unless the lake was rough, the Huron set their nets a mile or more from the island and they drew them in again at daybreak. They immediately gutted the whitefish, trout, and sturgeon that they caught. If the weather was good, the fish were spread on racks made of wooden poles to dry; if not, they were smoked and packed in bark containers. Some of the whitefish were boiled to extract oil from them. This oil was stored in gourd containers and was used to garnish food during the winter. If a number of fishing cabins were erected close together, the men of each took turns feasting and entertaining the others in the evening.

A few weeks after the whitefish season was over, the Huron went to catch *einchataon*, a fish of uncertain identity that was used to flavor corn soup. This fish was not gutted, but was hung in bunches beneath the roofs of the longhouses, where it remained edible throughout the winter. At other times of the year large schools of lake herring (*auhaitsiq*) were taken in nets. Entire communities cooperated in catching these fish, each person carrying away his share in large wooden bowls. Some of these fish were eaten fresh; the rest were smoked. In the winter, fish were caught through the ice. This was done with a net passed by means of a pole from one hole to another; the holes being arranged in a circular fashion.

Hunting was considerably less important than fishing from a nutritional point of view, although animal skins were necessary for clothing. More important, hunting was an activity that was much enjoyed by Huron men. Birds such as the geese and the great blue heron were hunted with the bow and arrow or were caught with nets. Often this was done in the fields, where large numbers of them gathered when the corn was ripe. Some birds, such as crows, were not eaten. Wild turkeys were common in certain areas, particularly southwest of the Huron setttlements near the Tionontati.

Because of the demands of so large a population, most game animals appear to have been hunted out in the regions adjacent to Huronia. As a result, meat was scarce or unobtainable during much of the year and skins for clothing often were in short supply. Hunting expeditions had to travel a considerable distance south or east of Huronia in order to find game. Most of the hunting took place in the fall, the hunters staying away for a month or more, but returning to their villages in time for the winter festivities. War parties returning from the Iroquois country also hunted in the region north of Lake Ontario. Again in late winter hunting parties made up of several hundred people journeyed several days beyond the borders of Huronia to slay deer. Women are reported to have gone along on some of these expeditions, probably to help butcher the game and carry home the skins and meat. They do not appear to have joined the autumn hunts, possibly because enemy raiders were still active at that time of year.

The principal game and the animal the Huron enjoyed hunting most were deer. These animals were hunted by large groups of men and were mostly taken in drives. Sometimes several hundred men would land on an island or form a line through the forest between one bend in the river and another. Then, making a loud noise, they would drive the animals toward a fixed point along the water. As they passed through the line into the water, the deer were either shot with arrows or killed with sharpened poles by men in canoes. On other occasions, the hunters built a triangular enclosure, open on one side but enclosed along the other two with barriers of brush up to 9 feet high. The sides of these enclosures were over half-a-mile long and at the narrow end they led into a pen from which the deer were unable to escape. Twenty-five men could construct such an enclosure within less than ten days. When it was finished, the hunters lined up before dawn at the open end and beating sticks together, they drove the deer into the pen at the far end, where they killed them with arrows. Repeating this every second day for thirty-eight days, a band of hunters was able to kill 120 deer. The skins and fat of the deer were carefully preserved, but only a little of the meat was taken back to Huronia to be used in feasts. Evidently, the main objective of these hunts was to obtain skins. The cold weather was useful because it preserved the meat and allowed the hunters to haul the skins back to their villages on sleds.

The other principal game animals were beaver and bears. Bears were tracked with specially trained dogs, then shot with arrows. The meat was preserved for feasts, but the entrails of the bear were fed to the dogs as a reward. Killing a bear sometimes required tackling the animal at dangerously close range, and various remedies were prescribed for bear bites. Beaver were usually hunted in the winter, since they remained in their lodges at that season and their fur was of better quality than in the summer. A hole was chopped through the roofs of their houses and they were killed when they were forced to come up for air. In the summer beaver were sometimes caught in nets. Beaver meat was eaten by the Huron, either fresh or smoked, and even before the beginning of the fur trade their skins were valued for clothing. The incisor teeth were used for woodworking. Muskrats as well as beaver were hunted by the Huron.

The Huron also hunted a wide variety of smaller animals, the bones of which have been preserved in the middens of archaeological sites. Rabbits were caught in snares, and tortoises were collected and eaten. A large-sized variety of mouse which infested the villages was also eaten.

Hunting and fishing were both the focus of many ritual activities designed to protect the hunter and bring him luck. Men frequently sought the advice of shamans or guardian spirits before starting out. Some fasted for a week or more and cut themselves so that the blood flowed profusely. This was done to invoke the aid of a man's guardian spirit and other spirits associated with the chase. Sometimes the aid of a spirit was sought by shaking a tortoise-shell rattle. While hunting and fishing, the Huron were careful not to burn the bones of any fish or animals or to let the fat of animals drop into the fire. They were also careful that the bones of animals were not thrown to the dogs. They feared that the souls of the animals they killed might report such maltreatment to living animals, who as a consequence would not permit themselves to be taken. The Huron also believed that fish did not like the dead; hence they were careful to keep their nets out of sight of human corpses and they did not go fishing when one of their friends had died.

When strong winds prevented the Huron from setting their nets, they would observe various rituals to assure good fishing. Tobacco sometimes was burned or thrown into the water to appease the spirits. Each cabin of fishermen on the islands in Georgian Bay had a "fish preacher," a man believed to be endowed with special powers to speak to the fish and attract them into the nets. Men believed to possess such powers were highly valued. One shaman announced that in order to assure large catches of fish, the Huron should give him presents and that at the start of the fishing season and while it lasted those planning to fish should burn tobacco in their fires in honor of his guardian spirit. Many of the villages complied and fishing was good that year. The Huron also noted that two of the principal chiefs of a village that did not send him presents were drowned on the lake during a thunderstorm, while they were returning from fishing.

Huron men also relied on charms to make them lucky in hunting, fishing, trading, fighting, gambling, and in love. Some charms had the power to confer many benefits; others were useful for only one purpose. Charms were highly valued and were inherited from one generation to the next. In some cases a new charm was revealed to a man in a dream. If a hunter found an animal difficult to kill and later found in its entrails something unusual, such as a stone or a snake, he would keep what he found in the hope that it would bring him good fortune. Likewise, stones that had a curious shape were kept since it was believed that these stones belonged to a spirit who lived in the woods and had lost them there. Some charms were obtained in trade from neighboring tribes, especially from the northern Algonkians, who were believed to possess especially powerful ones, possibly because they were renowned as hunters and fishermen. These charms were extremely expensive and are described as the most costly merchandise of the country. Men carried their charms about with them in their pouches. From time to time they spoke to them or would offer them a few beads or a bit of tobacco as a present. They also gave feasts to make their charms more powerful and invoked their aid with special songs.

The Huron claimed that some of their hunting and fishing customs were of Algonkian origin. Among these was a ceremony in which two girls who had not yet reached the age of puberty were married to the spirit of a fishing net. This ceremony, which was said to insure good fishing, was reported to have begun among the Algonkians when the spirit of the net appeared to a man in a dream asking for a bride to replace the wife he had lost. The ceremony then spread to the Huron. In return for consenting to the marriage, the girls' families were given a special share of the season's catch. The marriage apparently lasted only for one year.

While the protective rituals may reflect the dangers involved in hunting and fishing, those designed to bring good luck, especially in hunting, seem out of all proportion to the economic importance of these activities. While some of these customs were of Algonkian origin, many others were probably survivals from a time when hunting and fishing were much more important to the Huron subsistence economy than they were in the historic period. The continuing ritual importance that was accorded these activities may be part of an effort to reinforce the importance of traditional male activities. More will be said about such reinforcement in the next chapter.

Tame Animals

The Huron kept large numbers of dogs, who lived with them in their houses. Dogs were given names, and the Jesuits were annoyed that they were permitted to eat at will out of the cooking pots and that women allowed puppies, in the same way they allowed their children, to suck food out of their mouths. Some dogs were used in hunting, and dog meat was in special demand at feasts. Dogs were often sacrificed and eaten in Huron rituals, where they frequently appear to have symbolized a human being. Some dogs were very much loved by their owners, who would not permit them to be sacrificed in this way. A man who loved a particular dog very much often transferred its name to another when it died. Bears were also kept for sacrifice. These were usually young animals captured after their mothers had been killed by hunters. Such bears were given names and were kept for several years in a small round enclosure within the longhouse, where they were fed the leftovers from the meals. Some people kept tame birds either as pets or for eating, but this practice was not common.

Manufacturing

In spite of the Hurons' numbers and their interest in trade, their economy remained basically very simple. Few, if any, distinctions were drawn between the manufacturing of goods for household use and for trade. There were no full-time specialists, and every able-bodied adult was engaged in the production of food. Each household, consisting of a number of nuclear families, seems to have been an independent unit of production. Clear distinctions were drawn between men's tasks and women's tasks.

Besides cooking and tending to other household chores, the women ground the surplus corn into meal, which was traded for meat and skins with the northern Algonkians. The women also wove mats out of reeds and corn leaves, which they used to cover the doors and sleeping platforms of their houses. These mats were apparently not colored, like those of the Algonkians. Women also fashioned baskets out of reeds and birchbark and sewed together birchbark bowls from which to eat and drink. They made fiber out of the Indian hemp they collected and rolled it into twine on their thighs. The men used this twine to manufacture snares and fishing nets, a task that was performed during the winter months. Other textile work that was produced by the women included scarfs, collars, and bracelets, which were worn by both men and women. Samples of cloth with a twined weave have been found at the Jesuit mission of Saint-Marie and at the site of Ossossane. Women also scraped and softened animal skins and made clothes, game bags, and tobacco pouches from them. The skins were cleaned with small chert scrapers, and much of the sewing was done with bone awls and pieces of sinew. The skins were decorated with painted designs and with dyed porcupine quills, which were popular prior to the arrival of glass beads from Europe.

The women also made the globular pottery vessels that were used for cooking. To produce these, clay was dried and pulverized, then mixed with a little powdered gneiss to temper it. Water was added and the clay shaped into a ball. A hole was made in the ball with a fist and enlarged with the help of a wooden paddle to form the globular body of the pot. The pot was provided with a somewhat constricted neck and a low rim that was sometimes castellated.[2] The pot was dried in the sun and later fired in an oven.

These pots ranged in size from tiny vessels to ones a foot or more in diameter. Decoration was mostly confined to the lip and consisted of simple

---

[2] Castellated means the pot has one or more V-shaped projections around the rim. It has been surmised that these projections facilitated pouring (see Fig. 3).

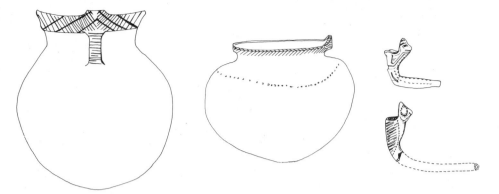

Fig. 3 Huron pottery. Left: two Huron pots. Right: two effigy pipes.

patterns made up of incised hortizontal, vertical, and oblique lines (Fig. 3).
Archaeologists assign the majority of sherds from historic Huron sites to three
pottery types: Huron incised, Sidey notched, and Warminster crossed; the first
two account for fifty percent or more of the sherds. These pottery types differ
from one another only in the shape of the lip and in the pattern of the incised
decoration. It is also worth noting that Huron pottery had only one functional
shape. This contrasts the variety and elegance of forms of pottery vessels found
in cultures of that period in the southeastern United States. Although Huron
pots could be set directly over a fire, they could not hold water for any length
of time without becoming soft and friable.

Pipes were also made out of clay, which was apparently shaped around
a grass core that burned away when the pipe was fired. Pipes were better made
than pottery vessels because the clay was either more carefully selected or better
fired. Many pipes were given a high polish, and sometimes a blackened surface
was produced by rubbing grease on the pipe, then letting it burn away (Kidd
1949:149). In addition to pipes with round or flaring bowls, the Huron
manufactured a wide range of effigy pipes decorated with human and animal
figures. According to Pierre Boucher (1664:101), it was the men who made pipes,
but it is uncertain whether he was referring only to pipes made of stone or to
clay pipes as well. The finest pipes are clearly the work of talented potters, and
it would appear that a limited number of people produced pipes for an entire
village. This may explain why pipes were treasured and why, when they were
broken, they were glued together with blood that the owner drew from his own
arm.

During the warmer months, when they could work out of doors, the men
built houses, constructed palisades around their villages, and fashioned canoes.
The largest canoes were about 20 feet long and 2½ feet wide and they held up
to six men. Smaller canoes were built for use on routes where there were many
portages. Even if they frequently leaked the light, but sturdy, canoes of the
Huron drew admiring comments from the French.

Winter does not appear to have been as much a time of leisure as
Champlain and Sagard say it was; instead, it was the time when people worked indoors. During the winter men wove fishing nets and probably made many of

their bows and arrows, snowshoes, sleds, clubs, and suits of wooden armor. Men probably also manufactured spoons and wooden bowls. At least one ladle has been found carved out of antler in the shape of a duck in flight.

Chisels and rectangular axes and adzes were chipped and ground out of hard stones such as diorite and granite, but the Huron rarely gave them a careful finish. Scrapers and drills were made of chert, and small, triangular projectile points were manufactured out of the same material. Other projectile points were made of bone. Bone was also used to make harpoon points. These had several barbs on one side and a perforation near the lower end. There were also various forms of bone awls and needles.

A variety of ornamental objects were probably also manufactured by men. Tubular beads were made out of bird bones and discoidal ones from the ribs of imported conch shells. Long beads that were square in cross-section, as well as ones in the form of turtles and other animals, were carved out of red slate. Pipes, some with effigy bowls, were carved out of stone, and combs and small amulets, some of the latter in human form, were whittled from bone.

Foreign Trade

It is clear that the key role that the Huron played in the French fur trade was an extension of their role as traders in prehistoric times. By the historic period, trade had become a source not only of luxury goods but also of meat and skins that were vital to a population that had outstripped the resources of its nearby hunting territory.

The chronic hostility between the Huron and the Iroquois seems to have made any regular trade between the two confederacies impossible. Occasionally, however, when there were negotiations, the Huron chiefs gave their Iroquois counterparts presents of beaver skins and in return received wampum beads, which they valued highly. In the historic period the Huron traded with the other Iroquoian tribes of Ontario. Although the Neutral probably obtained a certain amount of trade goods from the Iroquois, the Huron maintained a monopoly over the trade goods that were entering Ontario from the Saint Lawrence Valley. The desire of the Tionontati and Neutral to obtain iron axes and glass beads seems to have brought their former conflicts with the Huron to an end and promoted increasing trade among all the tribes of southern Ontario.

Most of the goods that the Huron sought to obtain in southern Ontario were luxury items. One of the most important imports was tobacco, which grew better among the Tionontati and Neutral than it did in Huronia. The Huron obtained black squirrel skins from the Neutral to manufacture cloaks that were much prized by the Algonkians and probably by themselves. The Neutral were probably also the source of robes made from *tiron* skins (*tiron* is a Huron word meaning wild cat or possibly racoon), which came from the Erie country, and of conch shells which came from the Gulf of Mexico. The latter were used to make beads. Sagard mentions that the Huron stored their fish oil in gourds that were obtained from a great distance, probably from the south.

A small amount of the goods that the Huron obtained from the northern Algonkians falls into the category of luxury items. These include winter clothing, often elaborately embroidered with porcupine quills, camping equipment, various kinds of charms, buffalo robes which came from west of Sault Saint Marie, and possibly native copper, since the Huron knew of the mines on Lake Superior.

The bulk of the trade with the north was in more basic items. To the northern hunters, Huronia was a source of cornmeal, which helped to keep them alive over the hard winters. Groups such as the Nipissing and the Algonkins from the Ottawa Valley wintered each year in the Huron country. In the middle of the autumn they began moving toward the Huron with the furs they had trapped themselves or collected from other tribes over the summer. On the way they stopped to fish on Georgian Bay, drying as many fish as possible, both for their own use and to trade with the Huron. When they reached Huronia, they set up their winter camps near the Huron villages. The Ahrendarrhonon appear to have been on particularly good terms with the Algonkin tribes from the Ottawa Valley, with whom their warriors were happy to fight and travel. It is probably because of this special relationship that the Ahrendarrhonon were the first of the Huron tribes to encounter the French along the Saint Lawence. The Nipissing are reported wintering farther west, among either the Ataronchronon or the Attignawantan.

The Huron did not bother to learn the languages of their neighbors, while their own language was a lingua franca among the Assistaronon, Winnebago, Ottawa Algonkins, and other Algonkian-speaking tribes with whom the Huron traded. The language situation, which seems to reflect the key role that the Huron played in the trading networks around the Upper Great Lakes, confirmed the Huron in their opinion that they were more intelligent than other tribes. Even the French were scorned for the difficulties they encountered in learning to speak Huron. The Attignawantan appear to have been particularly haughty in their dealings with the Algonkins and were mistrusted by them.

In addition to the trade that was carried on within Huronia, the Huron traveled north along the water routes of Lake Huron to trade with the Algonkians. These trips took some individuals as far as Lake Superior and Lake Michigan and into the central part of Quebec. In the winter the Huron crossed the ice of Georgian Bay to trade their cornmeal for fish among the nearby tribes.

There is good evidence that Huron traded with the northern hunters long before the arrival of the Europeans. While most of the goods that were traded are perishable and therefore difficult to trace in the archaeological record, pottery belonging to the Ontario Iroquoian tradition and dating as early as A.D. 1000 has been found in numerous Algonkian sites in northern Ontario. One of these is the stratified site at Frank Bay, which is probably Nipissing, but, were it not for the dog burials, might be considered Huron (Ridley 1954). Beginning around A.D. 1200, strong Ontario Iroquoian influences can be seen in the pottery, house types, and burial practices at the Juntunen site in the Straits of Mackinac (McPherron 1967).

Huron trade was governed by elaborate rules. The rights to trade along a particular route were said to belong to the family of the man who first pioneered it. No one was supposed to trade along that route without receiving permission from the head of the family who controlled it, and this permission was normally granted only in return for presents. If a man engaged in trade without permission, the master of the route and his supporters had the right to seize him and despoil him of his goods as he returned home. Once he was safely back in his village, however, they could only complain about his behavior.

The men who went trading did so both for profit and adventure. Traveling among foreign tribes was dangerous activity and served to test a man's courage. It also provided men with opportunities to enjoy themselves in various pursuits such as gambling with other tribes.

Although most of the trading seems to have been done by men in the prime of life, the major trade routes were under the control of leading chiefs. In Sagard's time, men from neighboring villages came to Khinonascarant to seek permission from chief Onorotandi to trade along the rivers and lakes leading to the Saguenay and from his brother Auoindaon to go to Quebec. Because the leader of the first Huron party to encounter the French was Atironta, the principal chief of the Ahrendarrhonon, the latter tribe could in theory have enjoyed the privilege of being the only Hurons to trade with the French. Either because they knew they could not defend their rights against the more powerful Attignawantan or because they wished to preserve good will with the rest of the confederacy, the Ahrendarrhonon agreed to share their trading privileges with the other three tribes.

Control over trade routes was an important means by which a man could acquire wealth and validate high status within his tribe. It is unclear to what degree lucrative new trade routes fell under the control of hereditary chiefs, thereby enhancing their power. Successful traders may have acquired personal renown and influence, but considering the nature of Huron political organization it seems unlikely that they would have been able to challenge the hereditary officeholders. The latter, on the contrary, were probably in a good position to acquire formal control over trade routes and to profit from this control. With the expansion of activity that followed the introduction of the fur trade the wealth of certain chiefs was probably considerably enhanced. This may explain the sobriquets *atiwarontas, atiwanens,* and *ondakhienhai* (big stones, elders, and stay-at-homes) that were applied to chiefs in the historic period.

The chiefs of the confederacy also attempted to control the number of young men who went out from the various villages in any one year to trade. This was allegedly done because a sufficient number of warriors had to be retained in the villages during the summer to protect them from Iroquois war parties.

The Huron took considerable pains to eliminate competition from rival traders. Only a few Europeans, such as Etienne Brule, sufficiently won the Hurons' confidence that they were allowed to travel with them into the far north. Even after the Huron concluded a treaty of friendship with the Tionontati, around 1640, they refused to let the latter share in their trade with the French. This is important because it demonstrates very clearly that the Huron confederacy was not merely a grouping of independent tribes that had agreed not to wage war against one another, as it is often claimed the Iroquois confederacy was at that time. The Huron confederacy was also a grouping of tribes that were willing to share in the same general trade and to protect this trade from outsiders. This reinforces the contentions that we have outlined above concerning the forces that molded the historic Huron settlement pattern.

Because the Huron valued their trade, they did not wish it to be disrupted, and therefore they carefully cultivated good relations with friendly tribes. In so doing, they were tacitly conforming to conventions that were understood and accepted by all the tribes in the region. Trading was embedded in a complex network of social relations, and the exchange of goods was often carried on in the guise of reciprocal gift giving. The Huron seem to have considered that reciprocity was an integral part of any kind of friendly or cooperative interaction, and ties between trading partners were regarded at least to a limited degree, as similar in kind to the ties that bound relatives together. Visits to foreign tribes were an occasion for feasts, speech making, and the formal exchange of gifts between chiefs. Such activities often occupied several days before and after the actual trading. Before entering the village of another tribe, the traders would paint their faces and put on their best ornaments.

This behavior at first puzzled the Europeans. They described the Huron as skillful traders and admired the manner in which they collected furs throughout large areas of northern Ontario and Quebec. Yet they also noted that the Huron scorned to haggle over the price of individual items and were annoyed at the French for doing so. While the Huron gave every sign of understanding market behavior, their actions were unnerving because they did not permit themselves openly to express a profit motive. What the French failed to realize was that the Huron success in trade depended to a large degree on their skills in maintaining good relations with those tribes with whom they traded, and in particular with the northern ones who had economies complementary to their own. This was done by extending hospitality to these people, by gift giving, and by the careful observation of various formalities. These were the conventions to which the French were expected to conform.

There was always the danger that if a Huron and someone from a friendly trading group got into a brawl and one of them was killed, the situation would lead to war between the two groups. Such crises were made even more serious because of the difficulty in finding someone to mediate the quarrel. It was, therefore, a Huron custom to pay more gifts to compensate for a murder of this sort than to compensate for the murder of one Huron by another. Champlain describes in detail a quarrel that broke out between the Huron and some Algonkin who were wintering near the Ahrendarrhonon village of Cahiague. The quarrel arose when one of the Algonkin chiefs decided to spare the life of an Iroquois prisoner that the Huron had given him to torture. The Huron, angered by this, sent one of their warriors to the Algonkin camp to kill the prisoner. The Algonkins, in turn, killed the intruder, whereupon the Huron took up arms and attacked the Algonkin camp, wounding the chief and pillaging the cabins. At this point, Champlain was called upon to be an arbitrator.

It also appears that the Huron sometimes exchanged their children with trading partners in other tribes. Such an exchange served as evidence of trust and goodwill and also provided hostages for the families involved. Some of these exchanges may have chosen to remain with their adoptive tribes, and this may account for some of the Algonkin women who are reported to have been married to Huron men. Trading partnerships may also account for references to Huron men having kinsmen among the Neutral and Tionontati, with whom they sometimes left their children.

Internal Economy

The average Huron wished above all to be loved and respected by his tribesmen and fellow villagers. His principal aim in acquiring wealth was to win affection by sharing it with others. Generosity was valued highly, and social status accrued to those who dispensed their possessions with an open hand. The acquisition of property was thus encouraged, although property was not accorded value as an end in itself.

This attitude toward property colored many aspects of Huron dealings with one another. The Huron did not have markets where they could gather to trade, and even ordinary barter does not appear to have been a favored means for the redistribution of goods within the confederacy. Instead, economic activities were largely incorporated within a system of social relations in which hospitality, gift giving, and ceremonial exchanges played an important part.

These attitudes encouraged a strong sense of communal responsibility. The Huron did not permit a villager to go without food and shelter. If a house and its contents were destroyed by fire, as not infrequently happened, the rest of the village helped its occupants to build a new one and presented them with corn, firewood, and household utensils to make good their losses. On one occasion all the households in Ossossane pledged to donate three sacks of corn each and whatever else they were able to help a number of orphans whose house had been destroyed. Visitors to a village were never refused food and lodging for as long as they wished to stay, although they were expected to give their host a present as a formal expression of their friendship and thanks. Families vied with one another to provide feasts and entertainment for their fellow villagers, to contribute to the communal treasury when funds were needed for reparations payments, and to give the presents that were required for religious reasons. These were usually given willingly since such generosity drew public acclaim and enhanced the donor's reputation. The raising of such funds was usually sponsored by the village council, and each present, along with its donor's name, was announced publicly. Presents were also publicly displayed at funeral and curing ceremonies.

The strong disapproval people had of stinginess also created feelings of guilt which helped to encourage generosity. A Huron who was particularly successful in hunting or trade feared that envious neighbors would seek to harm him or members of his family by means of witchcraft, and gift giving was seen as one way of averting this. Moreover, it was easy for the Huron to bring strong pressure to bear against anyone who refused to live up to their expectations concerning generosity. When Father Brebeuf was staying in the At-tignawantan village of Toanche, two fires ravaged the community, but spared the house that belonged to one of the village's wealthiest men. This led to considerable resentment, and there were threats from other villagers to set fire to this house as well. To counteract this jealousy, the owner of the house gave a feast to which the entire village was invited and turned over to his fellow villagers more than 120 bushels of corn. An individual who was consistently miserly and who refused to participate in village activities often was accused of being a witch, a serious crime since it exposed the accused to the danger of being slain.

Individual households produced most of the food and utensils which they themselves needed. As a result, there were no strong economic ties holding Huron society together. Individual households were capable of easily combining with or disassociating themselves from others. The unity of Huron society was largely based on shared ideals and mutual consent, not on economic necessity. Although some households were richer than others and their men were able to play leading roles in Huron society, these differences were not sufficiently great to encourage coercive forms of social control. Prestige was sought through public service and winning friends, not in the hoarding of property, which its owners were unable to protect. In this respect, the Huron did not differ from other stateless societies.

4

Warfare

H URON CULTURE was profoundly influenced by the warfare that prevailed
among the Iroquoian tribes of the Northeast. War was an inescapable
part of Iroquoian life and influenced every aspect of Iroquoian culture.
Huron subsistence patterns, social and political organization, and religious beliefs
can each be studied separately from one another. To understand fully the nature
of Iroquoian warfare, it is necessary to examine all aspects of Iroquoian culture
since they were all influenced by it.

Iroquoian Warfare

The French who visited Huronia were accustomed to wars that were
fought for territorial gain or commercial advantage or because of theological
differences. It is not surprising that when Champlain accompanied the Huron on a
campaign against the Iroquois, he thought that he was participating in a war
similar to those fought in Europe. Great was his annoyance when his Huron
allies, having traveled a great distance, were content to harass an Iroquois village
for several days before returning to Ontario to do their fall hunting. Champlain
considered the mission a failure and condemned the Hurons for their indiscipline
and lack of organization. He does not appear to have noticed that they showed
no sign that they considered the attack to have been a failure. Champlain obviously had failed to grasp the nature of traditional Iroquoian warfare.

After 1640, economic rivalry played an increasing role in warfare between
the Iroquois and neighboring tribes. This, plus a growing supply of guns and iron
hatchets, soon altered traditional patterns of warfare beyond all recognition
(Otterbein 1964). The information concerning Huron warfare prior to these
changes is thus our main source of data about the nature of traditional Iroquoian
warfare.

In order to understand Iroquoian warfare, a number of popular myths must be dispelled. It has often been stated that the warfare in early historic times was a struggle between the Iroquoian-speaking peoples and the Algonkians who lived east, west, and north of them. This idea evolved when it was believed that the Iroquoians had entered the Northeast only a few centuries before the Europeans. They were thus conceived of as a "disturbing cultural anomaly" that had forceably driven a wedge between Algonkian tribes that were indigenous to the area. This led the Algonkians to attempt to recover their lost lands and resulted in undying hostility between the two groups. The principal exception to this situation was the Huron, who strangely chose to trade rather than to fight with the Algonkians.

A careful examination of the evidence indicates that warfare tended to be chronic among the agricultural tribes of the Northeast, whatever their linguistic affiliations. Peaceful relations were maintained only if there were compelling reasons to maintain them, and trade was the most important of these reasons. Prior to 1615 the Huron and Tionontati had been at war and, as late as 1624, Sagard describes a Huron war chief trying to persuade the Huron to attack the Neutral. This suggests that until the development of the fur trade, the Huron were sporadically at war with the other Iroquoian tribes in Ontario. It is also a reasonable, if unproved, hypothesis that the peace that existed in historic times between the Neutral, on the one hand, and the Huron and Iroquois, on the other, was the result of the Neutral trading for European goods with both of these confederacies. In any case, there is no evidence that there was any more bitterness between the Iroquoians and Algonkians than there was between the various Iroquoian-speaking tribes and confederacies.

There is also no evidence that prior to when they obtained guns in large numbers the Iroquois were more warlike than the Huron or were militarily superior to them. The traditional struggle between these two groups appears to have been more or less an equal one with neither side seeking to annihilate the other.

Another idea that appears to be without foundation is that traditional Iroquoian warfare was a struggle between neighboring groups for additional land or hunting territories. This theory totally fails to account for warfare between the Huron and the Iroquois. Even if Iroquois attacks may have compelled some of the Huron tribes to settle in Huronia, their abandoned territory was not occupied by the Iroquois but remained part of the hunting territory of the Huron confederacy. There is also no evidence of a shortage of arable land in Ontario or New York State. Through time, the Iroquoian population tended to become concentrated in a smaller number of larger settlements, and, in Ontario at least, many areas of good farmland that had been populated in earlier times were abandoned as more tribes made their way to Huronia. There is no evidence of a lack of agricultural land even in Huronia, although there eventually might have been if the occupation of the region had continued.

While the Huron were at war with all of the Iroquois tribes, their principal adversaries were the Seneca, who lived nearest them. According to the Huron, this war had been going on for over fifty years. It appears to have been viewed as a prolonged blood feud in which each side killed members of the other in retaliation for previous killings. Since both the Huron and the Iroquois regarded such killings as further insults to be avenged, a state of continual conflict ensued. Families who had members slain in war or murdered by enemy raiders gave presents to their war chiefs to encourage them to attack the enemy. At the funerals of people who had been slain, the chief demanded that the wrong not go unpunished and that action be taken to see that the enemy was not tempted to strike again. There were occasional truces that were designed principally to facilitate an exchange of prisoners. These were sought to secure the release of important chiefs.

Waging War

Every man was expected to be a warrior as well as to be able to hunt, fish, and clear new fields. Boys were trained in the use of weapons from an early age and were encouraged to be brave, self-reliant, and uncomplaining. Men constantly sought opportunities to test their bravery. In order to become more nimble, they cut incisions in the fat of their legs and to gain courage they held burning sticks against their arms until the flesh was scarred. The highest ideal of a man was to demonstrate himself to be a brave warrior.

The Huron and the Iroquois did not wage war in the winter or in the spring and late fall when the leaves were off the trees and it was difficult to find cover. During the rest of the year, the Huron were on the alert for Iroquois raids, and rumors about enemy plans circulated from village to village. The larger Huron villages, especially on the southern and eastern perimeter of the country, were protected by palisades. While the latter were not as strong as the palisade that Champlain observed among the Iroquois, they were not necessarily a less effective means of defense. The Huron chiefs endeavored to keep a sufficient number of warriors at home during the summer to protect the villages and look after the women working in the fields. One of the techniques they used to do this was to spread rumors that an enemy attack was imminent.

The Huron chiefs also sought to cultivate friends among neutral tribes and even among the enemy who would give them advance warning of attack. These spies might be resident foreigners or even chiefs who for some reason were friendly toward the Huron. Such men were given presents by the Huron war chiefs out of public funds, but were expected to vouch for the truth of any information they supplied by sending a gift of some value along with it. The Huron dreaded traitors in their midst and tried to identify them so that they could watch them and kill them if they became dangerous. Because they feared a leakage of information, Huron chiefs were very circumspect about their own war plans, and, while they allowed visitors to enter and leave the country, they insisted that those they did not trust live in specially assigned houses and not travel about unattended.

The kind of campaigns that the Huron and Iroquois conducted against one another varied from year to year. Sometimes a band of several hundred warriors would lay siege to an Iroquois village. These men slowly made their way toward the Iroquois country, hunting and fishing along the way. After they crossed Lake Ontario, they hid their canoes in the forest and made their way on foot toward their objective, killing or taking prisoner any Iroquois they surprised along the way. The siege of a village might last a week or more. Fires were set along the palisade in order to challenge the enemy to come out and fight. When they did, the opposing sides lined up and fought a pitched battle. After there were a few deaths or injuries the enemy retreated into their village, taking with them any prisoners they might have captured. The Huron usually built a temporary fort near the village to return to at night, and they generally retreated before Iroquois reinforcements arrived from other' settlements. To protect their withdrawal the Huron stationed the old and wounded in the center and the young men who were well-armed at the sides and rear. The wounded were bound in a tightly flexed position and were carried home in baskets on the backs of their companions. Occasionally, the Huron invited the Susquehannock to join them in an attack on an Iroquois village.

If the Huron learned that a large Iroquois war party was approaching their country, warriors were sent out to ascertain the position of the enemy, while each of the villages strengthened its defenses until it was clear which village was going to be attacked. Then, depending on the number of the enemy, warriors came in from other villages to help to defend the one that was threatened. These warriors helped to man the palisades and discouraged the enemy by making a loud noise throughout the night.

Most years, five- or six-hundred young men set out for the Iroquois country. There, divided into groups of five or six men each, they hid in the fields or along paths in the forest hoping to capture a prisoner. At night more daring individuals would sneak into Iroquois villages, where they tried to kill some of the inhabitants and set fire to the houses. If possible, the prisoners were taken back to Huronia alive; if not, they were shot with arrows or clubbed to death and their heads or scalps kept as trophies. Scalps (*onontsira*) were tanned and in time of war were fastened onto poles and set up along the palisades of the villages to frighten attackers.

In order to prepare for these raids, a number of older and more daring chiefs traveled from village to village, explaining their plans and distributing presents to gain support for their project. These chiefs had the authority to determine where the warriors who fought under them would go and to dispose of the prisoners that were taken. The greatest support for their plans was found among young men. To demonstrate prowess in fighting against the enemy was the principal way for a young man to acquire prestige, and this made him anxious to fight. This was especially so because all of the important decisions affecting Huron life were made by older men. Young men were regarded as unproved and, therefore, as unreliable. The greatest opposition to war was expressed by the older hereditary chiefs, who claimed to fear the reprisals that would follow. Many of these chiefs also seem to have feared that gaining prestige in war would give the successful younger warriors a greater say in village affairs. Normally, the affairs of a village were managed by the heads of lineages and older men who were respected for their wisdom; in times of crisis power tended to pass into the hands of the leading warriors.

When support for an attack against the enemy had been gained at the village level, a general council was held at which the decision was confirmed. When the council was over, a war feast, which the women started to prepare for before daybreak, was celebrated. At the war feasts there was much singing and dancing. Led by some of the older men, the young warriors performed a dance in which, brandishing their weapons, they made their way from one end of a longhouse to the other. To show that they did not lack courage, the men chanted curses and abuse against the enemy and promised themselves victory. Under the pretext of doing it in jest, men would knock down others whom they did not like. At the end of the feast, the various war parties left to invade enemy territory.

The origin of the war feast was attributed to a giant whom a group of Huron encountered while living on the shore of a large lake. One of this group wounded the giant in the forehead because he failed to reply politely to his greeting. As punishment, the giant sowed the seeds of discord among this people and after recommending the war feast, another feast called the *Ononharoia*, and the cry *wiiiiii* to them he disappeared into the earth.

At the war feasts and while on the warpath, Huron warriors wore a circlet made of red moosehair around their heads. They also wore their finest necklaces and other ornaments. The reason given for wearing these ornaments was that if pursued, they could throw them behind them and escape while their adversaries stopped to pick them up. More importantly, however, they emphasized the ritual nature of war.

In war, as in hunting, the principal weapons used were a wooden club and the bow and arrow. Before the introduction of iron arrowheads, warriors covered their back, legs, and other parts of the body with a kind of armor made of thin pieces of wood laced together with cords. This armor was proof against arrows (Fig. 4). They also had shields made of cedar bark, some of which covered the entire body.

Each warrior carried with him a bag of roasted cornmeal that could be eaten without bothering to cook it or even soak it in water. A bag would feed a man from six to eight weeks, after which the warriors returned to their village for a fresh supply, unless they were able to forage along the way. Bands carried with them a pennant, consisting of a piece of bark fastened to the end of a long stick. This was painted with the emblem of their village or tribe. If the Huron found themselves trapped by the enemy, the older men would stay and fight while the younger ones attempted to escape.

Many warriors sought supernatural support to assure success and avoid capture by the enemy. Particular attention was paid to dreams. If the god of war appeared as a dwarf and caressed the dreamer or struck him on the forehead, this foretold a successful campaign. Songs that would assure success were also revealed in dreams. If a man dreamed that he was captured by the enemy, he would sometimes insist that his friends torture him to prevent the dream from coming true. One man who was so tortured was unable to walk for six months.

Shamans were also consulted before setting out for war. One shaman sang inside a sweat house while the warriors danced outside. Finally his spirit possessed him and he said that he saw the Iroquois coming from the south and

Fig. 4 A Huron warrior wearing slat armor.

predicted that they would be put to flight and many taken prisoner. Cheered by this news, the war party set out to meet the foe. Other shamans claimed to be able to tell what was happening far off and were consulted by people whose relatives were at war. One old woman was said to have done this by tracing the outline of Lake Ontario in the sand and setting small fires on either side to represent the Huron warriors and their adversaries. From the behavior of these fires, she claimed to be able to tell what was happening to the warriors at that very moment.

Treatment of Prisoners

During their stay in the Iroquois country, Huron warriors sought to perform acts of daring that would win the respect of their comrades and help them to acquire a good reputation back home. Nothing was as desirable, however, as to be credited with the capture of an enemy warrior. Women and children who were captured were usually tortured and killed on the spot. If they were taken back to Huronia, it was to be adopted into Huron families to replace relatives who had been slain by the Iroquois. Able-bodied men were rarely slain at once, unless the Huron had captured too many of them or found that they endangered their own security. From the moment of capture, most men became the victims of a sadistic game in which the hope of escape or of being returned to their own people was balanced off against physical pain and the greater likelihood of a savage, if glorious, death. In their treatment of prisoners, the Huron reveal a sinister aspect of the psychological finesse that was a very important part of their culture.

If the Huron came upon an enemy who was by himself, they surrounded him and said quietly, "*Sakien*" (sit down). His choice was to obey or be killed on the spot. In spite of the prospect of being tortured, most men preferred to surrender because they had hopes of escape or rescue at a later time.

As soon as the Huron had an enemy in their power, they tore out his fingernails and cut or bit off the fingers that he used to draw a bow. This often caused a serious infection, but rarely resulted in the prisoner dying before he reached Huronia. His neck and shoulders were cut with a knife and his arms bound with a special leather thong that warriors carried with them for this purpose. At the same time, the Huron made a speech to him about the cruelties that he and his people had practiced on them, saying that he must be content to suffer likewise. Then they made him sing his war song; each man had his own which he sang in time of danger. To show his courage, the prisoner often continued to sing all the way to Huronia. Meanwhile, he was well fed so that he might better endure the tortures that awaited him.

A single warrior received the credit for each prisoner that was taken. If several warriors claimed the same prisoner, the latter had the right to designate his official captor. A prisoner often named someone other than the man who was principally responsible for his capture. This would arouse the latter's jealousy, and sometimes he would secretly help the prisoner to escape rather than see the honor of his capture go to another. The possibility of getting his captors to fight among themselves was a source of hope for a prisoner.

While the capture of a prisoner enhanced the reputation of a warrior, it did not give him control over what happened to him. If men from several tribes had participated in a war party, they held a council of war on the way home in the course of which the prisoners were divided among them. Sometimes it was also decided to give a prisoner to the Algonkian allies as a friendly gesture. When each group of warriors returned to their respective tribes, they turned their prisoners over to the chiefs who had organized the raid, and these chiefs called tribal councils to decide what villages or clan segments should receive each prisoner. Feasts were also held to celebrate the victory. At these feasts, the warriors again performed their dances and chanted the praise of the "chiefs who had killed the enemy."

The prisoners were then led from one village to another until they reached the one to which they had been assigned. The treatment that different individuals received at this time varied. Some prisoners were dressed in fine beaver skins and were treated with much kindness at each village. Sometimes dog feasts were given in their honor. Most, however, were stripped and bound hand and foot. These prisoners were painted and had wampum collars placed around their heads to indicate that they were victims destined to be tortured. As they approached each village, their captors led them slowly between two lines of villagers, who delighted to torture them with clubs, thorns, knives, and fire-brands. Everywhere the prisoners were taken, they were expected to sing.

Each prisoner was eventually adopted by a family of whom a member had been killed by the Iroquois. The prisoner symbolically replaced the lost relative and served to dry the tears of the bereaved. Normally, prisoners were made available only to the leading families of any village. In one case a prisoner was turned over to an important chief of the northern Attignawantan village of Arontaen to replace a nephew who had been captured by the Iroquois.

This adoption was an important step in determining the prisoner's fate. If for some reason, his appearance, manners, or ability were pleasing to his adoptive family, they might decide to spare his life. Henceforth, he would be well treated and would assume the titles and possibly the name of the man for whom he had been given as a replacement. Like the Iroquois women and children who were brought to Huronia, he would gradually become a loyal member of his new family and in time might go to war with the Huron against his own people. The insecurity of the prisoner played an important role in his transformation. Even after this adoptive family decided not to torture him, there was the danger that if he displeased them in any way, they might still have him killed. Under these circumstances, the constant treatment of the prisoner as a lost relative must have encouraged him to identify with this role as his best chance of survival.

These happy adoptions were, however, quite rare. More often the caressing of the adopted prisoner was by torture. The village as a whole looked forward to such an event, and the battered condition of many male prisoners allowed their adoptive parents to explain that ordering their death was an act of kindness befitting a good parent.

Even after the prisoner's adoptive relatives had condemned him to die, they continued to treat him with courtesy and an outward show of affection. Although he was tied so that he could not escape, the women of the family wept when they fed him, and the men would give him their pipe to smoke, wipe the sweat from his face, and fan him if he were hot. By using the prisoner to recall their dead relative in as vivid a manner as was possible, the family was able to work up greater enthusiasm to avenge the latter's murder.

Very often the chiefs and old men of the village who were guarding the prisoner would talk to him about his capture and question him about what was happening among his people. This was done quietly, and no attempt was made to extract any information by torture. Before being slain, the prisoner gave an *athataion* or farewell feast similar to that given by any man who thought he was about to die. Everyone was free to attend the feast, the food being provided by the prisoner's newfound relatives and executioners. Before the meal began, the prisoner walked through the longhouse and in a courteous manner invited the Huron to amuse themselves in killing him since he did not fear death. Then he sang and danced the length of the house, with the Huron joining in. It was extremely important for a prisoner to behave bravely both at this time and throughout the gruesome torture that followed. Such behavior was not only evidence of his courage; it spelled future misfortunes for his tormentors if they could not compel him to weep and plead for mercy.

The torture of a prisoner might last for a single night or for as long as five or six days. The entire village and people from surrounding villages assembled to watch and participate in the event. In the evening these people assembled in the house of the principal war chief of the village, the older people mounting the sleeping platforms, the younger ones filling the central aisle below. Before the prisoner was brought in, the chief reminded those who were assembled that the torturing of a prisoner was an important act that was viewed by the sun and by the god of war. He also warned the villagers to be careful to burn only the prisoner's legs at the beginning so that he would not die before dawn. The concern that the prisoner should not die before sunrise was indicative of the sacred aspect of the torture that was to follow, the sun being the special witness of the fate of warriors. The sacred nature of the event was also emphasized by the chief's order that everyone should refrain from sexual intercourse that night and behave in an orderly and restrained fashion.

At this point the prisoner was led in. He was stripped of whatever clothes he still wore and his hands were bound together. It was announced to what chiefs the main parts of his body would be given after he had been killed. The prisoner was then forced to make his way back and forth from one end of the longhouse to the other, while all those who were present armed themselves with a brand or a burning piece of bark, which they thrust at him as he passed. To increase his torment the Huron also tried to force him to run through the hearths that were lighted down the center of the longhouse. At the ends of the cabin he was frequently stopped and made to rest on hot ashes taken from the fire. Here the bones of his hands were broken, his ears pierced with burning sticks, and his wrists burned or cut through by wrapping cords around them and pulling them back and forth as hard as possible. Later, fire was applied to his genitals. Sometimes, while a prisoner was making his way from one end of the longhouse to the other, he was able to scatter clouds of dust and ashes from the fireplaces or even to set the house on fire. In the resulting confusion, the prisoner had hopes of making his escape. While it is unlikely that any prisoner had much of a chance of fleeing the village, let alone of being able to make his way home, the thought that this was possible continued to sustain him. As the prisoner's strength failed him, he had to be carried through the longhouse. At this point the chiefs ordered the people to cease torturing him so that he could live until sunrise. The prisoner was then put on a mat and allowed to rest, while many people left for a breath of fresh air.

When he began to revive, he was forced to sing once more and his torture began anew. Prior to this time, the principal attacks had been aimed at the extremities of his body. These were designed to make him suffer, but were not meant to endanger his life immediately. Now, when the prisoner was no longer able to run about, torture was applied to the rest of his body, mainly by the youths of the village. They made cuts in his arms, legs, thighs and the other fleshy parts of his body, quenching the flow of blood by thrusting glowing brands into the wounds. His tormentors patiently waited their turn and showed no signs of anger or a lack of self-control. Their speeches were those of friends, but they were speeches of fearful irony. One youth would say that he was caulking a canoe for the prisoner, at the same time burning his body in imitation of the process; another would state that the prisoner was cold and proceed to warm him by roasting his flesh; still a third would protest that he knew nothing about torture, while committing some fiendish act that the Jesuits could not bring themselves to describe. In the course of this torture, every part of the prisoner's body was cut, burned, or bruised. From time to time, the Huron gave him something to eat and poured a little water into his mouth so that he would last through the night. During this phase of the torture, the Huron redoubled their efforts to make the prisoner cry out as much as possible. Occasionally, their mock benevolence wore thin and they taunted the prisoner, saying that he killed Huron thinking that retribution would not be forthcoming.

On the morning the prisoner was to die, fires were lighted before dawn around a scaffold 6 or 7 feet high that had been erected outside the village. The prisoner was led to the scaffold and tied to the branch of a tree that passed overhead in such a way that he was still free to turn around. The Huron enjoyed watching a prisoner play up to torture and at no time bound him so tightly that they could not observe his contortions. Once he was securely tied they continued to burn his body, but they also began to attack his vital organs. The prisoner was made to eat pieces of his own flesh, and brands were thrust down his throat and into his eyes and rectum. During this period he was prevented from sitting down by brands thrust through the platform from below. Later he was scalped and burning pitch was poured over his head. When it was clear that he was about to die, his head was either cut off or broken open with a club. At the same time, the Huron cut out his heart and chopped off his hands and feet. Then they cut open his belly and gave all of the children present small pieces of his bowel, which they hung on the ends of sticks and carried through the village as symbols of victory.

If the prisoner had been particularly brave, the Huron would roast his heart, which was eaten by the young men in an effort to acquire his courage. Some men also made cuts in their neck and let the prisoner's blood run into them since they believed this would prevent them from ever being surprised by the enemy. The prisoner's body was then cut up in order to be cooked and eaten. Some ate the body with horror; others relished the taste of human flesh. We are again dealing with an act that was primarily of religious significance.

After sunset on the day the prisoner was killed everyone made loud noises to drive his soul from the village. The souls of all warriors who had died bravely were considered dangerous, and it is not difficult to imagine why the Huron particularly did not want the souls of their victims to remain in the village.

Analysis

The three themes that motivated Iroquoian warfare are reasonably clear. First, it was the principal means by which young men acquired personal prestige. Second, it was the way in which injuries inflicted by members of one tribe or confederacy on another were avenged: War was merely blood revenge on a large scale. Third, Iroquoian warfare was stimulated by religious ideals. Through it prisoners were obtained who were sacrificed to the sun or the "god of war" by torturing them to death. These three themes were woven together in such a way that each one complemented and reinforced the other (Trigger 1967). The acts of daring that Huron warriors performed in enemy territory provided them not only with satisfaction for similar acts committed by the enemy against their own people but also with a supply of captives for sacrifice. The method of sacrifice, in turn, provided the Huron with an opportunity to vent their hatred of the enemy on a particular victim, and gave the victim, as warrior, a final and glorious opportunity to display his courage.

Blood revenge was probably common in the Northeast from earliest times. It seems likely, however, that as the people of the Northeast become more dependent on their crops, warfare increased in intensity. Cooked human bones begin appearing in sites in Ontario around A.D. 1300 and are most frequent in sites dated between 1450 and 1500 (Wright 1966:64, 91). If these findings also apply in New York State, they constitute an index of the rise and gradual decline of cannibalism, and, quite likely, of the sacrificial cult, in the Northeast.

John Witthoft (1959) has argued that as corn agriculture replaced hunting as the dominant mode of subsistence, the resulting decline in the role of men as food producers led them to seek more prestige as warriors. At the same time, women projected their resentment at the lack of male participation in routine tasks by transforming their traditional role as butchers of game into a new one as butchers of male captives. This theory has two main weaknesses. First, it ignores the importance of fishing to the Iroquoian economy and also the important and arduous work performed by men in clearing new fields, a task that was probably far more difficult than planting and tending the crops. Second, men as well as women played an important and active role in the torture of prisoners. Public tortures and executions were not unusual spectacles in seventeenth century Europe, and thus this aspect of Huron culture did not surprise European visitors as much as one might expect. What did surprise and horrify them, however, was that women should participate actively in such proceedings; hence, perhaps, came the emphasis that was given to the role of women in their description of the torture of prisoners.

In spite of these qualifications, there appear to be some basically valid points in Witthoft's analysis. In early times, hunting probably did serve as the principal measure of a man's courage and his ability to use weapons. Fishing and clearing fields required energy and devotion, but such activities do not appear to have provided Iroquoian men with an opportunity to acquire an appreciable amount of prestige in relationship to one another. Thus the lessening importance of hunting may well have been an important factor promoting a growing interest in war. The apparent decline in warfare after 1550 may reflect the growth of confederacies, which served to suppress local warfare. The conflicts that continued between the confederacies seem to indicate, however, that by then warfare was basic to the social organization of all the northern Iroquoian peoples. This is probably because it was the principal means by which men gained personal prestige and established a role for themselves in the social and political life of their communities.

The savagery with which prisoners were tortured may partly be a projection of hostilities that were generated within Huron society. It may also be attributed to the tensions that were produced by the constant menace of death which threatened all the Iroquoian peoples as a result of endemic warfare. While the search for revenge and individual prestige appear to be indigenous aspects of warfare in the Northeast, the sacrificial cult contains numerous elements derived from the southeastern United States, and ultimately from Mesoamerica (Knowles 1940; Rands and Riley 1958). These traits include the sacrifice of prisoners, the removal of the heart, the killing of the victim on an elevated platform and in view of the sun, and the cooking and eating of all or part of the body. While there are important differences between the sacrificial cult as it was practiced in the southeastern United States and among the northern Iroquoians, these differences merely indicate that the cult did not diffuse in its entirety from one region to another. Instead, certain key ideas seem to have diffused from the south and were used by the peoples of the Northeast to develop a sacrificial complex of their own.

5

Kinship and Family Life

THE EXPLORERS AND MISSIONARIES who described Huron life were familiar with the government and customs of Europe, which they regarded as conforming to the natural order of society. There is no evidence that these men gained any clear insight into the formal structure of Huron society. The traders, although they had dealings with many of the leading men in Huronia, perceived them as individuals rather than within the context of their society. Even the Jesuits, in spite of their long stay in Huronia, tended to be aware of those features of Huron life that most resembled their own. Soon after their arrival in Huronia, they realized the importance of villages as units of social, political, and economic interaction. However, they never showed much interest in Huron tribal structure, although it was clear to them that the various tribes reacted differently to their missionary activities. Finally, there is no evidence of their being aware of the Huron clan system or that the Huron kinship system was different from their own, in part because they avoided living in the same cabins as the Huron whenever possible. Only a few inadvertent references to these institutions can be gleaned from the seventeenth-century accounts. In order to interpret these references, we must turn to descriptions of the Wyandot and Quebec Huron at a later date as well as to descriptions of Iroquois social structure. The comparisons with the Wyandot assume that in these aspects the Huron and Tionontati cultures were much the same.

Clan Structure

Every Huron was simultaneously a member of one of four tribes and one of possibly eight clans. The tribes were political units. Each one was made up of one or more villages and had its own territory. The clans were fictive kinship[1]

---

[1] Fictive kinship is claimed kinship without evidence of biological descent. Such claims are frequently made to facilitate social or political interaction, especially in societies where kinship is of great social importance.

groupings, the people belonging to the same clan (or to clans having the same name) claiming descent from a common female ancestor. Clanship had no territorial implications, and members of the same clan apparently were found living in many villages and among all the Huron tribes.

An individual was a member of the same clan to which his or her mother belonged. The Wyandot clans were exogamous, and it is likely that the Huron clans were also, at least ideally. Thus a Huron's father and mother generally belonged to different clans. This may add structural significance to Brebeuf's statement that Huron parents paid special attention to marriage as a means of linking different families together.

The clan seems to have played its most important role at the village level. The members of a community who belonged to the same clan appear to have constituted a well-defined grouping of considerable social and political importance. For convenience, we may term these local groupings *clan segments*. It is uncertain, however, whether clan segments were lineages whose members could accurately trace their descent from a known common ancestor or whether they were larger fictive groupings. The Hurons' lack of interest in genealogies, however, strongly suggests the latter. Every clan segment that was of any size had its own chiefs, who managed the internal affairs of the segment and represented it on the village, tribal, and confederacy councils. Because these offices were clan privileges, a chief could not transmit his position to his son, the latter not being a member of his clan. Instead, his office was passed on to one of his sister's sons. The clan segment was the primary unit responsible for protecting members from harm and securing reparations for injuries done to them.

Some of the small villages may have been composed of a nucleus of individuals who belonged to the same clan segment. The larger villages, however, were made up of a number of clan segments. In the latter it appears that each clan segment had not only its own chief but also its own section of the village. Individual segments remained independent enough so that they could split away from a village and found a new community of their own if they felt their members were being unjustly treated. When villages like Khinonascarant or Cahiague split apart to form two or more new villages, it is likely that the cleavages were along clan segment lines. Likewise, there are examples of small villages, containing perhaps only one clan segment, joining together to form a large multisegment village.

Regrettably, the most obscure aspect of our knowledge of clan segments concerns their residence patterns. The individual Huron household rarely consisted of a single nuclear family; usually an average of six nuclear families lived together in the same longhouse. It has generally been assumed that among all the northern Iroquoian tribes, a normal household consisted of a mother and her daughters, or a group of sisters, living together with their husbands and children. This statement gains a certain measure of support from several sources. Pierre Boucher (1664:103) stated that Huron men went to live with their wives. However, other things that he wrote about the Huron reveal a far from perfect knowledge of their social organization. Brebeuf observed that a woman exercised lifelong jural authority over her daughter, and a small number of the households that are described in the Jesuit relations seem to conform to a matrilocal residence pattern.

The idea that Huron residence was matrilocal is also attractive because it conforms to the general theory that matrilineal descent develops as a response to such a residence pattern rather than the reverse (Schneider and Gough 1961: 551–554, 659–660). The only possibility of an alternative is that the Huron and other Iroquoian groups may have borrowed matrilineal institutions from elsewhere without borrowing matrilocal residence patterns as well (Schneider and Gough 1961:660–661). The most common interpretation states that matrilineal residence developed when women assumed a dominant role in food production. It is argued that the work teams of greatest economic importance in Huron society consisted of a woman and her daughters, whose cooperation in growing crops constituted the basis for forming common households. This theory ignores the economic importance of male activities such as fishing and forest clearance, which probably required even more cooperation than did the work of the women. The origin of extended family households and of their matrilineal bias may ultimately be demonstrated to pose separate problems for Huron culture history. If feuding has as great an antiquity as it appears to have, the need for protection may have been one important factor promoting the development of extended family dwelling units. Male activities tended to keep men away from their villages and in scattered groups for much of each year, while the women remained at home in daily face-to-face contact. This situation, combined with the higher mortality rate among young men than women, due to war and accidents, may have encouraged the formation of matrilocal households as the most stable form of extended family.

In spite of this situation, the matrilocal view of Huron society has certain defects in terms of the evidence that is available. The offices in a clan segment were held by men who belonged to that segment. Thus, if a man regularly went to live with his wife's relatives, officeholders would have been prevented from living among their followers. Moreover, the majority of Huron households that are described in detail appear to be ones in which the women were living with their husband's relatives (Richards 1967). There is also considerable evidence of married women living outside the village of their birth.

The ideal solution would seem to be a pattern of avunculocal residence, whereby a young man, after he reached a certain age, went to live with his mother's brother. In this way an extended household, although matrilineal, would be made up of a man and his nephews rather than a woman and her daughters. There is, however, no positive evidence that such a custom existed among the Huron. Even if it did, it may have been limited to the lineages of chiefs. These are the sort of families whose members the Jesuits seem to have known best. Finally, we must question whether the Huron had any strict rule of residence or whether this depended on factors such as the amount of space that was available and the rank and personal preferences of the married couple. No satisfactory answers are likely to be forthcoming from the available data. All that we can do is to note that on both theoretical and substantive grounds the traditional picture of the Huron and Iroquois household can be accepted only with considerable reserve.

If we assume that the five or more Turtle clans that were recorded among the Wyandot during the last century are subdivisions of a single original clan, the Wyandot appear to have once had eight clans: Turtle, Wolf, Bear, Beaver, Deer, Hawk, Porcupine, and Snake (Connelley 1900). In the nineteenth century, the Huron of Quebec claimed that they had formerly consisted of four tribes each divided into five clans: Wolf, Deer, Bear, Beaver, and Turtle (Wilson 1885). Possibly the existence of the three others had been forgotten. It is significant that the Seneca, Cayuga, and Onondaga also had eight clans and that these clans were named after the same animals as were those of the Wyandot, except for Porcupine and Snake, which were replaced among the Iroquois by Snipe and Heron.

An oblique reference to the eight Huron clans may be found in the account of the gifts that were presented to the Jesuits in 1648 to compensate them for the murder of a lay assistant. These presents were made by chiefs representing the "eight nations" of the Huron. In this context nation is probably a translation of the Huron word for clan. This interpretation is especially attractive because among the Iroquois it was the clans that were responsible for settling blood feuds.

Nothing is known for certain about the origins of the Huron clan system. Huron accounts of the development of their society strongly suggest that the clan segments originally were autonomous hunting bands,[2] although a number of adjacent bands may have recognized a common ethnic or tribal affinity. Later, a number of clan segments joined together to form the larger Huron villages (Tooker 1968). The recognition of an affinity between clan segments that had the same name or symbol, and with it the development of the clan system, may have come about with the development of effective political organization on the tribal and confederacy level. It is always possible, however, that the clan system of historic times was built on some kind of naming system that had influenced the designation of bands in the Northeast at an earlier period.

There is no evidence prior to 1650 that the Huron clans were grouped together to form phratries[3] or moieties. The Wyandot evidence suggests that they formed three divisions or phratries, which like the clans themselves may have been theoretically exogamous. The phratry organization, if it existed, seems to have been purely of ritual significance.

Kinship

Our sources provide us with very little information about the Huron kinship system. Nowhere is there any evidence that the French were aware that the Huron used kin terms differently from themselves. This makes it difficult to

[2] Needless to say, these bands need not have had the same rules of descent as the Huron clan segments had in historic times.

[3] A phratry is a cluster of clans linked together by ceremonial functions. The term is reserved for societies having three or more clusters. When there are only two divisions, the term "moiety" is used.

determine whether, when they appear in the Jesuit *Relations*, terms like father or brother are being used in the French sense or as translations for Huron terms that covered a wider range of kinship relations. It was not until 1724 that Joseph Lafitau attempted to describe the Huron-Iroquois system of kinship terminology. Most of what can be said about the operation of the Huron kinship system is an extrapolation from what was observed among the Wyandot in the nineteenth century (Morgan 1871:291–382).

In his dictionary, Sagard lists the following Huron kin terms: father, *aystan* or *aihtaha*; mother, *anan* or *ondoüen*; son or daughter, *ayein*;[4] brother or sister, *ataquen*; younger brother, *ohienha*; grandfather, *achota*; uncle *houatinoron*; aunt, *harha*; nephew or niece, *hiuoitan*; niece ("manière de parler aux femmes"), *etchondray*; cousin, *earassé*; father-in-law, *yaguenesse*; son-in-law, *aguienhesse*; brother-in-law, *eyakin*; sister-in-law, *nidauoy*. These terms are, for the most part, very similar to later Wyandot ones and suggest that the two kinship systems worked in approximately the same manner.

Like other Iroquoian systems, Wyandot extended the term for mother (*ahnǎ'uh*) to include mother's sister and used the term for father (*hiese'tǎ*) for father's brother. Mohawk, Cayuga, Onondaga, and Oneida had a special term for mother's brother, but used the word mother for father's sister. The Seneca and Wyandot had special terms for both mother's brother (*häwäteno'rä*) and father's sister *(ahrä'hoc)*. Parallel cousins[5] were called brother and sister; the word cousin *(järä'seh)* being reserved for cross-cousins.[6]

A man referred to the children of his sister, female parallel cousins, and female cross-cousins as his nieces (*yashonedrä'ka*) and nephews (*hashonedrä'ka*); the children of his brother, male parallel cousins, and male cross-cousins were called his sons (*aneah'*) and daughters (*eneah'*). In the case of a woman the situation was reversed; children of sisters and other female consanguineal relatives[7] of the same generation were called sons and daughters, while the children of male consanguineal relatives of that generation were called nieces (*ewä'teh*) and nephews (*hewäteh*). All consanguineal relatives of the second ascending generation were called grandfather (*häshutä'*) and grandmother (*ahshutä'*) and those of the second descending generation were called grandson (*hatra'ah*) and granddaughter (*yatra'ah*). There were separate terms for older and younger brother (*haye'uh/ hayea'hä*) and older and younger sister (*aye'uh/yayeah'hä*). A situation apparently unique among the northern Iroquoians was the Wyandot use of the term "father's

---

[4] Apparently Sagard did not detect the subtle differences in their terms for son and daughter, brother and sister. Note the Wyandot terms supplied later.

[5] The term "parallel cousin" is applied to father's brother's child or mother's sister's child. Cousins are parallel when the parental siblings through whom they are related are of the same sex.

[6] A cross-cousin is a first cousin, the child of father's sister or mother's brother. Cross-cousins assume importance in anthropology because they often fall outside the common prohibition on marriage with parallel cousins and because they are sometimes designated as preferred or prescribed mates.

[7] A consanguineal relationship is based on descent from a common ancestor (as opposed to affinal relationships based on marriage).

sister" (*ahrä'hoc*) to refer to mother's brother's wife and the reciprocal use of the term "mother's brother" (*häwäteno'rä*) for father's sister's husband.[8]

The matrilineal principles that governed clan membership, the inheritance of offices, and perhaps residence are not strongly reflected in Wyandot kinship terminology. In a person's parental generation, kinsmen of the same sex who are members of the same clan are terminologically distinguished from members of other clans. In ego's own generation, however, cross-cousins and parallel cousins are distinguished from one another, no attention being paid to whether they are on the father's or mother's side. In the next generation, the distinction between classificatory[9] sons and daughters and nieces and nephews depends on whether their parents have the same or the opposite sex from ego. The sex of ego also determines the terms that are used for niece and nephew. Sex linkages appear to account for a great deal in this system, while lineage and clan membership seem to count for much less. This suggests that the Wyandot kinship terminology reflects a bilateral rather than a unilineal social organization. Bilateral tendencies are also evident in the prohibitions against marrying consanguineal kinsmen within several generations on either the mother's or the father's side. To what degree these bilateral tendencies in Huron (and Iroquois) kinship behavior are a reflection of an earlier social organization is a matter for speculation. As we have seen already, however, even in historic times bilateral relationships may have been more important than Morgan's classic description of Iroquois culture suggests.

Houses

The typical Huron longhouse, or *ganonchia*, was a windowless structure 20–30 feet in width and about the same in height. Archaeological evidence indicates that most longhouses were between 90 and 100 feet long, the length being related to the number of families that inhabited them. Houses were constructed of slabs of bark tied onto a wooden frame and held down by a network of saplings. Cedar bark was considered to be the best covering, although it was extremely inflammable and often caused conflagrations that destroyed entire villages.

The Huron normally aligned their houses so that one end was facing northeastward into the prevailing winds. It has been suggested that this was done to protect houses from being blown down by the strong winds coming off the lake. It also appears to have lessened the danger of fire spreading from

---

[8] Although the Huron had separate terms for father-in-law and mother-in-law, this terminology suggests that at some time they may have practiced cross-cousin marriage. This pattern has been documented among bilateral and patrilineal Algonkian-speaking groups such as the Naskapi, Cree, Ojibwa, Ottawa, and Algonkins. Eggan (1966:104) has suggested that possibly early Iroquois social structure was based on cross-cousin marriage. He suggests that this form of marriage represents one way of solving certain problems that beset small-scale groups living in difficult environments and with a low-level technology.

[9] Classificatory kinship terminology is characterized by the merging of terms for lineal and collateral kindred (for example, a single term for father and father's brother).

one house to another since the wind would tend to drive the flames along a single house rather than towards others. The length of the houses made it necessary to align a number of them side by side in order to conserve space. These groupings of houses may roughly reflect the clan structure of the village. Houses were normally kept three or four paces apart in order to minimize the danger of fire spreading from one to another. They were also set back from the palisade that surrounded the village to make it easier for the warriors to defend the settlement. Some of the larger villages may have had open spaces in the center where public gatherings could assemble, but these do not appear to have been as carefully laid out as some of the early French sources indicate. Most of the important Huron celebrations appear to have taken place indoors or in the clearings outside of villages.

The precise construction of Huron longhouses is not described in the French sources. Some authors have suggested that they consisted of a framework of poles stuck upright in the ground which was covered over with a gabled or semicircular roof in the manner that Morgan describes for the Iroquois. Lalemant says, however, that bent poles formed the walls and roofs of Huron houses. This suggests that they were built of poles that were driven into the ground, then bent over and lashed together to form the roof (Fig. 5). Cadillac (Kinietz 1940:41, 42) describes the Wyandot as building houses in a similar manner less than fifty years after the dispersal of the Huron. The main poles were fastened together with wooden crosspieces, and the whole structure was covered with bark. Archaeological evidence indicates that these houses were rarely rectangular in outline; the ends usually were rounded. Doors were located at the ends, and sometimes along the sides, of the longhouses. Holes were left in the roof to permit smoke to escape and to let in light. If more room was needed, the length of the house was increased by adding onto one end of it.

Not all Huron longhouses conformed to a single pattern. Prehistoric ones have been found that are much wider than the houses the Jesuits describe (Channen and Clarke 1965). These houses had a row of stakes running down the center to support the roof. Similar rows of poles are reported from the reputed site of Saint Ignace II.[10] A considerable amount of variation in Huron house patterns probably remains to be documented archaeologically.

Brebeuf states that at least one house in each village was deliberately made larger than the rest. This house belonged to a leading chief and was the main place where feasts were held and meetings took place. In at least some villages there were two such houses. One belonged to the leading war chief, the other to the leading civil chief. The house of Atsan, the war chief who lived in the Attignawantan village of Arontaen, was called *otinontsiskiaj ondaon*, "the house of cut-off heads" and was the place where the main councils of war were held and where the prisoners who were brought to the village were tortured. Domestic affairs were discussed in *endionrra ondaon*, "the house of council."

The exteriors of Huron houses were decorated with paintings, mostly done in red. Some of these may have indicated clan or lineage affiliations; others seem

---

[10] Saint Ignace II was the Huron village where Fathers Brebeuf and Gabriel Lalemant were killed by the Iroquois. Concerning the claims of the site to be Saint Ignace II, see Heidenreich 1966:125.

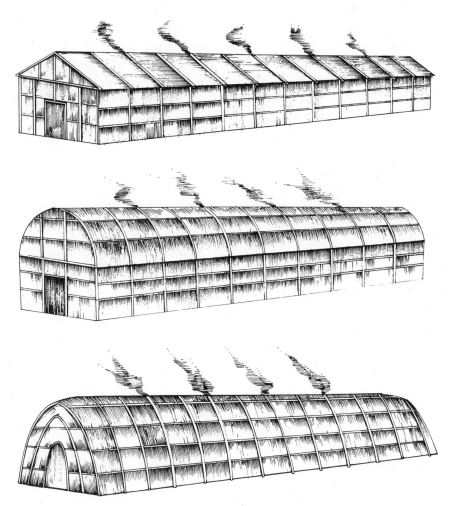

Fig. 5 Top and center: alternative reconstructions of Iroquois longhouses. The upper reconstruction is based on an illustration from Morgan's Houses and House-life of the American Aborigines; *the center reconstruction is based on John Bartram's diagram of an Onondaga longhouse of 1743. This house is similar in construction to others found farther south.*

Below: a tentative reconstruction of a Huron longhouse, following Lalement and Cadillac.

to have been done for pleasure. At either end of the longhouse was an enclosed porch, where corn, firewood, and other possessions were stored. The corn was kept in large bark containers. Near the center of the house were two large poles, which held the racks on which the pots, clothing, and other possessions of the occupants were stored. Down the middle was a row of fireplaces, each about 20 feet apart. One family lived on either side of each hearth. Sheets of bark covered the ground along both sides of the longhouse and over this, running the entire length of the structure, was a bark platform, well supported and raised 4 or 5 feet off the ground. In the winter, when the Huron slept on the lower level near the fire, these platforms served as a canopy. In the summer, if they did not sleep in the open air, they slept on top of these platforms to escape the fleas. There is no evidence whether or not there were bark partitions between the fire-places, but evidently there were few opportunities for any family to enjoy much privacy.

The French were much surprised by the cooperativeness and friendliness of families living under these crowded conditions. Although the Huron manifested a great deal of hostility toward their enemies, their behavior in their homes and villages was noted for its gentleness and tranquility. Brebeuf commented at length on the love and unity that existed among them and on their kindness to one another in the face of poverty, sickness, and death. Peace and friendship appear to have been more common among the Huron than they were in France. The Huron were famed for their generosity. Any visitor to a village unless he came from a hostile tribe was welcome to food and lodging. When a stranger arrived at a cabin, his host lighted a pipe and, after smoking it himself, passed it to him as a sign of welcome. If food was being served, it was offered to the guest. No invitation was required to stay in any cabin, and a guest was normally welcome to stay as long as he wanted. A concern not to offend others made the Huron punctilious in visiting one another and attending feasts and dances. They were not easily annoyed and usually concealed wrongs that were done to them rather than making a public show of anger. Living in communal houses and in large crowded villages, the Huron obviously strove to keep disruptive behavior to a minimum and sought to channel their aggression along carefully controlled lines.

Although the seventeenth-century French were more inured to discomfort and unpleasant odors than most modern anthropologists are, they did not find Huron longhouses attractive to live in or visit. In particular, they complained about smoke, crowding, vermin, and dogs. In spite of the care that the women took to gather wood that was dry and smoke-free, not all of the smoke from their fireplaces escaped through the holes in the roof. Because of this, eye diseases were common and many older people became blind. When more light was needed, small torches were made out of conical rolls of birchbark. Attempts to work with defective lighting inside the houses in wintertime must have added considerably to the eyestrain. Because of the danger of fire, the Huron placed their most valued possessions in boxes and buried them in shallow pits, both inside and outside their houses. Mice and fleas were common in the houses, the latter no doubt because of the large number of dogs that were free to roam about. Women periodically drove the lice from their furs and from their bodies. As they did so they caught and ate them.

Huron houses were sparsely furnished. Reed mats covered the doorways and were used to sit and sleep on. The Huron may have had special skins to cover themselves in the winter, but they are usually said to have muffled themselves at night in the clothes they wore. The benches running along either side of the house served as chairs. Most work was done seated either on these platforms or on the floor.

Fig. 6   Huron woman grinding corn.

Cooking

Cooking was a woman's job and was done at the family fireplace inside the longhouse. At least some hearths were probably kept burning all the time in order to avoid having to make fire. When this was necessary, it was done by rubbing one stick inside the hollow of another. The Huron normally took two meals a day, one in the morning, the other in the evening, although they would eat informally at other times of the day. Corn was the main item in their diet. After the kernels had dried they were either pounded into flour in a mortar hollowed out of a tree trunk using a pole 6–7 feet long (Fig. 6) or else ground between two stones. Afterward, the husks were removed with bark fans.

Although the Jesuits comment on the variety of Huron dishes, their cuisine consisted of a number of variations on a few themes. The most common dish was a thin soup made of cornmeal boiled in water. This soup eliminated the need to drink water separately. It was varied by adding slices of fish, meat, or squash. The fish were put into the pot whole and after being boiled for a time were removed, pounded into a mash, then returned to the pot. No attempt was made to remove the bones, scales, or entrails. At special feasts a thick corn soup was prepared and served with some fat or oil on top. Soup was also made from roasted kernels of corn mixed with beans and from *leindohy*. The latter were small ears of corn that were allowed to ferment for several months in a pool of stagnant water. The Huron regarded *leindohy* as a delicacy, an opinion not shared by their French guests.

The Huron also ate unleavened bread, which they baked under the ashes. To give it more flavor, dried fruit and pieces of deer fat were sometimes mixed into the dough, which was fashioned into small cakes an inch or more long. These cakes were either wrapped in fresh corn leaves, if the latter were available, or else stuck directly into the ashes. If the latter procedure was followed, the bread was washed before it was eaten. In the summer, special bread was made from fresh corn, which the women masticated, then pounded in a large mortar. The soft paste that was produced was wrapped in corn leaves and then baked.

The Huron also roasted ears of corn and slices of squash, and they cooked *leindohy* in this fashion. They also roasted fish and meat. In the summer, they enjoyed sucking the juice from ripe cornstalks. They did not use salt, but occasionally added some ashes to their soup.

Childhood

Children were welcome in Huron society and were much loved, especially by the women. Families were small, at least by comparison with those in France. The average seems to have been about three children per family. This figure resulted in part from a high rate of infant mortality but also because women abstained from sexual intercourse for two or three years while they breastfed each child. The Huron are said to have rejoiced more at the birth of a girl than of a boy. This may reflect a matrilineal tendency in Huron society; however, it may merely indicate the value that the Huron placed on women as childbearers. The Huron wanted many male and female descendants to care for them in their old age and to protect them from their enemies.

A variety of taboos was associated with pregnancy. It was believed that if a pregnant woman looked at an animal her husband was stalking, the animal could not be taken. Likewise, if she entered the house of a sick person, he would become worse. However, the presence of a pregnant woman was believed essential for the successful extraction of an arrow, according to a ceremony that was practiced by the Wenro.

Women generally continued to work up to the time of their delivery and tried to be on their feet again as soon as possible afterwards. When a woman was about to give birth, a corner of her cabin was partitioned off with a few skins. Some were attended by an old woman who performed the functions of a midwife; others delivered themselves. Woman attempted not to cry out in childbirth for fear of being thought cowardly and failing to set an example for others. It appears that just as a man proved his courage in battle, a woman proved hers by giving birth to a child. It was no easy task, and a considerable number of women died in childbirth.

The mother pierced the ears of her newborn child with an awl or fishbone and stuck a quill or some other object through them so that the holes would not heal shut. Later, beads and other trinkets were hung about the child's neck;

whether or not they were amulets is uncertain. Some mothers also made their children swallow grease as soon as they were born.

Sagard states that the Huron had a large supply of names available to give their children. It is possible that, as among the Iroquois, particular names were the property of different clans and the custom was to give the child one of the clan names that was not in use at the time. If a man assumed a new name upon inheriting an office, he passed his original name on to some other relative.

During the day, the baby was kept on a cradleboard about 2 feet long and a foot wide. The cradleboard was often decorated with small paintings and strings of beads. The baby was swaddled in furs in such a manner that an opening was left for it to urinate through. In the case of a girl a corn leaf was used to carry off the urine without soiling the child. A soft down, perhaps that of cat-tails, was used in place of diapers. The cradleboard was often stood up on the floor of the lodge. When the mother wished to carry the child with her, the cradleboard either was hoisted onto her back by means of a tumpline or was propped up inside her dress in such a way that the child could look forward over her shoulder. At night the child slept naked between its parents.

While the mother was still breastfeeding her child, she began to give it pieces of meat she herself had masticated. If a mother died before a child was weaned, the father attempted to feed it by filling his mouth with corn soup and then having the child swallow the liquid.

Nothing in Huron culture shocked the French more than their failure to use physical punishment to discipline their children. All of the sources agree that children were never struck, and this, in the opinion of the French, resulted in children showing little respect for their parents. Children frequently went without clothing and even in winter roamed out of doors scantily clad. According to Sagard, this hardened them and accounted for their robust constitutions in later life. Boys refused to help their mother to draw water or perform other household tasks. From an early age they were trained to use the bow and spent much of their time outdoors shooting arrows, learning to use the fish harpoon, or playing ball games or snow snake (making a curved stick slide over the snow). These activities helped to forge strong and enduring links between boys of the same age. It has been argued that for men these ties became more important than those of family and kinship. The training of young girls was quite different. Girls learned to pound corn at an early age, and as they grew older, they played games that taught them to perform household tasks. When a girl reached puberty, she was not required to leave the house while she was menstruating, as were the women in neighboring Algonkian tribes. Henceforth, however, she cooked the food she ate separately during these periods. Women made small pots for this purpose.

There is some evidence that, at puberty, at least some young men went on a vision quest. One boy, about fifteen years old, went into the forest where he fasted, drinking only water for sixteen days. Then he heard a voice from the sky telling him to cease his fast and an old man appeared to him. The old man announced that he was the boy's guardian spirit and that the boy would live to an old age and have four children. Then he offered the lad a piece of human flesh and a piece of bear fat. The boy ate the latter and thus became a successful hunter. In later years he stated that had he eaten the human flesh that was presented to him in his vision, he would also have become a successful warrior.

Marriage

Men and women were formal and restrained in each other's presence. Kissing and embracing in public was not permitted, even for young people. Indirect evidence suggests that the Huron, both married and unmarried, tended to have sexual intercourse outside the village. This secured a certain amount of privacy that was not possible in the crowded longhouses. It also probably introduced a considerable amount of seasonal variation into the annual birth cycle.

In spite of this prudery, premarital sexual relations were considered normal by the Huron and were indulged in soon after puberty. To the dismay of the French priests, girls were as active as men in initiating such relationships. The French also commented on the lack of sexual jealousy among young people and the gentility with which these activities were carried out. Young men did not fight over girls and accepted that the latter had a right to refuse their advances. Sometimes a young man and woman entered into a fairly long-standing but informal relationship with each other, in which case the girl became known as the young man's *asqua* or companion. Such a relationship did not, however, prevent either partner from having sexual relations with other friends.

Young people do not appear to have had sexual intercourse with individuals whom they were not eligible to marry. Unfortunately, our knowledge of Huron rules concerning the choice of marriage partners is extremely limited. The Huron were monogamous, and Sagard says that they did not marry any relative within three degrees of consanguinity. This rule apparently applied on both the paternal and maternal side of the family. In addition, they do not appear to have been allowed to marry any member of the same clan. Bressani reports that men often married their dead brother's widows, and Charlevoix says that this custom and that of a man marrying his deceased wife's sister were rigidly adhered to by the Huron and the Iroquois. There is no additional evidence, however, to confirm this.

The Huron did not attach the same importance that we do to the distinction between being married and unmarried. Instead they recognized various stages of experimentation and growing commitment between a man and a woman that did not culminate in a stable relationship until children were produced.

While parents could not compel their children to marry, they played an important role in arranging marriages. Parents often suggested a suitable girl to their son and, if he was agreeable, they provided him with a present to offer her and approached her parents to seek their support for the match. The consent of the girl's parents was necessary for any marriage to take place. When these preliminaries met with success, the boy painted his face and, putting on the finest ornaments he owned or could borrow, he went to the girl and offered her his present. The latter might consist of a beaver robe or a wampum necklace. If the girl accepted the present, the boy came and spent a number of nights in succession with her. During this time the two had sexual intercourse but did not speak to one another. After this, the girl could either reject her suitor or agree to marry him, but in either case she kept the presents he had given her. Some girls displayed with pride the presents they had collected from numerous rejected suitors. If the girl agreed to marry, her father provided a feast to which the relatives and friends of the two families were invited. When all were assembled, the girl's father, or a master of ceremonies, announced the reason for the gathering and invited the guests to enjoy the feast. The woman now became the man's *atenonha*, or wife.

A girl's parents sometimes objected to a marriage on the ground that the young man was not a good warrior, hunter, or fisherman and hence was incapable of looking after her. Young couples who were unable to obtain the permission of the girl's parents to marry sometimes ran away together, while well-disposed relatives tried to change her parents' minds. If a young girl who had many lovers became pregnant, it was normal for each of these men to claim the child was his and for the girl to choose from among them the man that she wished to be her husband.

A marriage could be terminated at the desire of either partner. Prior to the birth of a child, infidelity and divorce seem to have been common, but afterwards married couples rarely separated. In spite of, or perhaps because of, the freedom that had prevailed until this time, sexual relations between a husband and wife do not seem to have played a vital role in holding marriages together. Although adultery was not a legal offense, husbands do not appear to have indulged in it in any conspicuous way, although for several years after the birth of each child they were unable to have intercourse with their wives. Men spent long periods away from their wives each year, and the Jesuits reported with interest marriages that had held together in spite of the husband being rendered permanently impotent as the result of illness. If couples who had been married a long time quarreled or were temporarily separated, friends and relatives would intervene to save the marriage.

In spite of the relative stability of these mature marriages, the Huron took the right of divorce seriously. One of the most common reasons that middle-aged men gave for not becoming Catholics was the danger of their wives leaving them and being unable to remarry. In spite of the clan system, children sometimes stayed with their fathers after a divorce, although others were retained by their mothers.

6

Government and Law

THE THOUSANDS OF HURON who lived south of Matchedash Bay had not only a subsistence economy but a social and political organization that permitted a far larger number of people to live together and cooperate than was the case among the hunting bands that inhabited the Canadian shield. By 1610, the Huron confederacy had grown to embrace four main tribes and many villages. The larger villages each contained several clan segments. The main factors that had promoted the growth of the confederacy appear to have been trade and, possibly to a lesser extent, wars with the Iroquois.

The confederacy effectively suppressed all blood feuds among its members. This permitted the Huron to live side by side, to cooperate in their common defense, and to share a lucrative trade with the north. The unity of the Huron was not a temporary development brought about by the personality of an outstanding chief; instead, it was founded on a well-defined system of government with a careful division of powers among the different levels of social organization. At least some important tribal and confederacy offices were hereditary within certain lineages. In this way, the interests of the various tribes and clan segments were protected, while the activities of these groups were coordinated with one another in the general interest.

In spite of the size and complexity of the Huron confederacy, nothing about its organization shows any sign of being a radical departure from the ideas about government that prevailed among the smaller scale societies of the Northeast. This suggests that the confederacy was an indigenous development out of the Iroquoian institutions of earlier times. Each household remained economically self-sufficient, and clan segments were willing to brook little interference in their internal affairs. Moreover, disagreements and disputes between clan segments, villages, and even tribes do not appear to have been uncommon. The Huron confederacy did not have the power to curb these tendencies; instead it had to attempt to resolve each crisis as it arose. Government, whether at the village, tribal, or confederacy level, strove to achieve a balance between the integrative and divisive forces inherent in Huron society. The confederacy respected the rights of its constituent clan segments, villages, and tribes and solicited only enough support from these groupings so that it could act for their common good. While it was a fragile structure built on compromise, it was able to cope with the political challenges that confronted the Huron people prior to the arrival of the Europeans.

Chiefs

The French are in agreement that the Huron recognized two principal kinds of chiefs. The Huron terms for these appear to have been *garihoüa andionxra* and *garihoüa doutagueta*.[1] The first were civil chiefs who were concerned with problems of peace and everyday life. These chiefs negotiated all foreign treaties, settled disputes and arranged feasts, dances, and games. The second were war chiefs, who were concerned exclusively with military matters.

Being a chief was burdensome in that it required time and the expenditure of considerable wealth. Chiefs were expected to entertain their followers as well as to provide hospitality for visitors. Chiefs also often had to travel considerable distances to attend meetings, sometimes in very bad weather. The chief at whose house the meeting was held had to provide food and entertainment for his visitors. These expenditures were, however, offset by the presents that chiefs received for services they performed and from their ability to profit from the control of trade routes.

It is generally believed that among the Iroquois only the offices of sachems, or civil chiefs, were hereditary in particular lineages. Arthur C. Parker has stated, however, that war chieftainships were held by the same lineages that had sachemships (Tooker 1964:43). The French sources strongly suggest that among the Huron each clan segment (*famille*) had two chiefs (*capitaines*), one for peace and one for war. Thus in the larger villages there were several civil chiefs and several war chiefs, representing the various clan segments of which the village was composed.

The civil chieftainships were hereditary in particular lineages, the office passing from a man to one of his brothers' or his sisters' sons. Since there was no rule to determine which individual within a particular lineage should inherit the office, personal qualities seem to have counted for a good deal. The lineage members selected the new chief and in doing so they considered the qualifications of the candidates. These included their intelligence, oratorical abilities, wealth, popularity, and perhaps above all their performance as warriors. Individuals who did not wish to play an active part in village life might refuse the offer of a chiefship at this stage. This was important since chiefs who failed to perform the duties expected of them could be dismissed at any time by their lineage or clan.

---

[1] This is not the explanation of these terms Sagard gives in Wrong 1939:149. In his "dictionary," however, *garihoüa andionxra* is defined as "capitaine pour la police" and *garihoüa doutagueta* as "capitaine pour la guerre." *Outaguetés* was the Huron word for war, and *andionxra* may have meant "council" (compare with *endionrra ondaon*, "the house (*ondaon*) of the council").

The investiture of new chiefs appears to have taken place in the spring, apparently at the annual meeting of the confederacy council. The main event of this ceremony was to confer on the new officeholder the ceremonial name of his predecessor, which henceforth he used as his personal name. Thus the name of a man holding a particular office remained the same from generation to generation and, while in effect a personal name, served as a title. This practice indicates the strong emphasis that the Huron placed on structural continuity in their political organization. Obviously, such continuity was considered more important than historical or genealogical considerations. A chief was expected not only to assume the name of his predecessor but also to exhibit the same personal qualities.

Prior to an investiture, a magnificent feast was given. The chiefs who attended were well fed and were provided with rich presents to win their support for the candidate. After his election was approved by the various chiefs of the confederacy, his new name was conferred on him. The new chief was further identified with his predecessor by being symbolically drawn from the grave by the assembled chiefs. The chiefs then presented him with gifts on behalf of all the clan segments, villages, and tribes they represented. Each present was accompanied by a stereotyped statement of its symbolical import. Presents were given to draw the deceased from the grave, to give him weapons to repel his enemies, and to make the earth solid under his feet so that it would remain immovable during his tenure of office. Two women, probably the senior women of his clan segment, were expected to attend the investiture, and if they did not, this was felt to betoken misfortune for the officeholder.

New chiefs were given special insignia of office, which the French did not describe but which they said were regarded as the most treasured objects in the country. These regalia were passed on from a chief to his successor. In addition, a chief had a package of council sticks (*atsatonewai*), which functioned as the books and papers of the country. Tooker (1964:47) has suggested that these were mnemonic devices that served a purpose similar to strings and belts of wampum among the Iroquois. Sometimes, however, these sticks were buried with the dead.

After the investiture, there was a magnificent feast of celebration. At this time, the old men recited the traditions and myths of the Huron so that the young people could hear and remember them. Following this celebration, the new chief recruited some young men to go on a war expedition with him. His aim was to perform some daring exploit that would make it apparent that he had inherited not only the name but also the powers of his predecessor.

The French report that the relatives of these chiefs served them as assistants and counselors. At least one of these assistants may have been a deputy who frequently accompanied the chief and made public announcements in his name. The counselors attended the various meetings and consultations by means of which a civil chief managed the affairs of his clan segment; these were probably the heads of the lineages and households which made it up. In coming to decisions at this level the opinions of all the older men seem to have been considered very seriously.

The mode of election of the war chiefs and their role in the government of Huronia is not well understood; nor is it clear to what degree this position, like that of the civil chiefs, was hereditary within a certain lineage in each clan segment. There is a tendency to believe that valor must have played an important part in qualifying a man for this position; hence it was more likely to be assigned on the basis of individual performance than to be passed down through a particular lineage. This view, however, overlooks the fact that all men were warriors and that success as a warrior was important for acquiring renown and qualifying for any position. It seems quite possible that this post, like that of the civil chief, was the property of a particular lineage within each clan segment. Some of the war chiefs were old men, so there is no reason to believe that this was a position that was quickly passed on from one successful warrior to another. Quite possibly it was a position held for life.

If Huron political organization resembled that of the Iroquois, only the civil chiefs had seats in the main tribal and confederacy councils. These seem to have met at regular intervals and were responsible for maintaining order within the confederacy and peaceful relations with other tribes. Councils of war are known to have been held, however, at the village, tribal, and confederacy levels and these were probably attended by the war chiefs of the various clan segments. In Arontaen, the house of the leading war chief of the village served as a meeting place for these councils. When greater security was felt necessary, meetings were held at night in secret places in the forest. Sometimes the representatives of various other tribes who also were at war with the Iroquois were invited to attend these meetings. Around 1637 the Jesuits were being asked to attend war councils as the representatives of the French.

Huron chiefs had no formal powers at their disposal to coerce their followers. Moreover, the Huron were sensitive about their honor and intolerant of external constraints. Overbearing behavior on the part of a chief might in the short run produce a violent reaction and lead to fights within or between lineages. In the long run, chiefs who behaved arrogantly or foolishly tended to alienate support and finally were deposed. The ideal Huron chief was a wise and brave man who understood his followers and won their support through his generosity, persuasiveness, and good judgment.

The French were at first puzzled, then intrigued, to see a government maintaining law and order among many thousands of people without the aid of a police force, imprisonment, or capital punishment, all of which were regarded as essential in their own society. It would be interesting to know how much the Jesuits' comments about this aspect of Huron political organization contributed to the development of the idea of the natural goodness of man that later became an important tenet of the rationalist philosophical tradition.

The enforcement of a chief's decision often depended on his securing the support of public opinion and bringing this to bear against refractory individuals. The support that a skillful chief could acquire in this way was quite considerable. The Jesuits recount that on one occasion when a young man struck a well-known chief, the whole village rushed to the chief's aid and were restrained only with great difficulty from killing his attacker on the spot. Moreover, we shall see that in spite of the meager formal powers that chiefs had at their disposal to coerce their followers, many of them were able to amass considerable informal powers.

Many men who were neither civil chiefs nor war chiefs acquired a reputation for bravery, sagacity, or generosity and this served to enhance their influence in the community. In later life, the opinions of these men came to carry considerable weight in the affairs of their village or their tribe. While these prestigeful individuals were known collectively as the Old Men, the more outstanding among them were called chiefs. The possibility of being recognized as an outstanding individual, even if no clan office was available, was a great encouragement to young men to excel in subsistence activities, trade, and war.

Village Government

Fenton (1951) has stressed the importance of the village as a unit of Iroquois social and political organization. Much of what he says applies equally to the Huron. Villagers were involved daily in face-to-face interaction with one another and this created a special concern about each other's behavior that is not found at the tribal or confederacy level. Part of this was an intimate concern with their fellow villagers' physical and psychological welfare. Villagers helped one another to build houses, aided those who were in distress, and shared in the tasks involved in defending the village. They also participated in many feasts and collective rituals and joined societies whose membership crosscut their clan affiliations. Finally, in the large villages intermarriage among the different clan segments helped to forge strong bonds of community solidarity. Similar, although weaker, bonds served to connect the smaller villages to the large central towns. The village seems to have been as important in Huron myths and folklore as it was among the Iroquois.

The principal chiefs in each village were the civil chiefs and war chiefs of the clan segments. In the large villages there might be three or more chiefs of each kind. Because these chiefs represented clan segments, they could not be removed from office except by their own clansmen. In theory, no chief seems to have been recognized as superior in rank to any other, but in practice one of the civil chiefs was recognized as being the head chief of the village. It is unclear whether the clan segments in a village were ranked in order of importance and the chief of the senior clan segment automatically became head chief or whether this depended upon the personal qualifications of the individuals concerned. The prestige of various civil chiefships tended to rise or fall depending upon the performance of the incumbent. No doubt the size of the various clan segments also played an important role in determining the relative importance of the various chiefships within the village.

The village councils were made up of the clan segment chiefs of the village as well as the Old Men. While the title of the latter group suggests that it consisted of all the senior men in the village, it is likely that only those individuals who had acquired a considerable amount of prestige participated in these councils.

The village council seems to have met frequently, perhaps even daily, to discuss village affairs. Often there was little business to transact, and the meeting took on the characteristics of an old boys' club. The meetings were normally held in the house of the head chief. At more formal meetings, the head chief sat in front of a fire while the other chiefs and the Old Men formed a circle around it. When everyone had arrived, the doors of the house were closed and those present sat for a time quietly smoking their pipes. The smoke was believed to provide them with clear insight into the problems at hand. Then, if there was business to be discussed, the head chief announced it in a loud, clear voice and those who had any opinions to express did so. Those who did not speak but were believed to have something to contribute to the discussion were asked for their advice. Discussion usually continued until some kind of consensus had been worked out. Although anyone present could express an opinion, the older and more important men controlled the council. Any public announcements resulting from the deliberations of the council were made by the head chief or his deputy.

At these meetings matters that concerned the village as a whole were discussed. The decisions of the counselors influenced many areas of social life. It was they who arranged public feasts, dances and lacrosse matches and who decided for whom special curing rites, requiring general village participation, would be performed. The latter work was facilitated because many of the men who played a leading role on the village council also held important positions in the religious societies. In addition, the council undertook to see that none of the families in the village was in need and coordinated communal projects such as building houses and palisades. All legal disputes between people who belonged to different clan segments within the village were adjudicated by the village council. Because all of the clan segments, as well as the more important lineages, had members on the council, the interests of all the major groups received due consideration.

While the literature states that legal disputes that arose between inhabitants of different villages were regarded as affairs involving all the members of both villages, Tooker (1964:52) has pointed out that among the Iroquois these were clan matters, and she has suggested that on this point the French sources may be in error. According to her interpretation, if a dispute were between members of two segments of the same clan, it would be regarded as a clan affair; if it were between members of clan segments belonging to different clans, it would be settled by representatives of the two clans involved. If segments belonging to both clans lived in the two villages, their crosscutting loyalty to clan and village would have created an ideal atmosphere for settling the dispute.

It seems to me, however, to be highly unlikely that the Jesuits were in error about the general sense of what they were observing, even if they did not perceive clearly the role of clanship in Huron society. Clans (as distinguished from clan segments) were part of the ideal structure of Huron society; villages were a concrete social reality. In most villages the various clan segments probably felt that they had more in common with each other than with segments of the same clan in other villages. When a clan segment found itself at odds with a clan segment in another village, it is likely that the other clan segments in the village rallied to its aid and even may have made contributions toward any reparations payments that were necessary. Such action would have contributed greatly to the solidarity of the village. It is doubtful whether, with the exception of the clan segment itself, any other solidarity was considered more important.

Each village is reported to have had a stock of furs, wampum, and other goods that were at the disposal of its chiefs. These goods were obtained either as donations from members of the community or from peace treaties, exchanges of prisoners, and from legal settlements with other groups. One of the chiefs was appointed to look after these goods, which were used for various purposes such as seeking the support of other groups for making war, making public presents at the investiture of chiefs, and making the payments involved in settling disputes with other groups. If the supply of goods became exhausted, contributions were called for and, as it was considered evidence of public spiritedness to donate to this fund, such calls rarely went unheard.

Occasionally there were general meetings attended by all the men of the village about twenty-five years old and over. These meetings were summoned by a special call. It seems unlikely that these were legislative meetings. More likely they were assemblies at which announcements of general interest to the village were made and where questions could be asked. It is noteworthy that no women or young men attended either the village council meetings or these general assemblies. Whatever power women may have had was wielded behind the scenes. Politics was a man's business; the focus of a woman's interest remained within her family and household.

Tribal Government

Because the Tahontaenrat all lived in one village, their tribal and village governments probably were identical. Each of the other tribes had a council that was apparently made up of the chiefs of the clan segments from its various villages. One of these chiefs was recognized as the principal chief and spokesman for the entire tribe, and the tribe was often referred to by his name. The word *enondecha* meant, alternatively, chief, tribe, and district. It was apparently this tribal chief whose permission foreign groups had to obtain if they wished to cross his territory. This was usually granted in return for a present.

Sagard reports that the principal chief of the Attignawantan had the name of Auoindaon and lived in the village of Khinonascarant. After 1623, this village declined in importance, and by 1636 Anenkhiondic was said to be the head chief of the Attignawantan. He lived at Ossossane, which by that time was clearly the most important village of the Attignawantan. Auoindaon remained the most important chief among the northern Attignawantan, and the rivalry between him and Anenkhiondic seems to reflect the general division within the Attignawantan that we noted above. Endahiaconc, the principal chief of the Attingueenongnahac, was also the head chief of the village of Teanaostaiae. The principal chief of the Ahrendarrhonon was Atironta. He was the first Huron chief to encounter the French and, because of this, he and his successors were regarded by the Huron as the special allies of the French.

In spite of the importance that the French and the Algonkians attached to the head chiefs of the various Huron tribes, it would be a mistake to regard their position as being similar to that of a European head of state. Although the members of a particular tribe shared a common territory and had common traditions, they seem to have viewed themselves politically as being a collection of clan segments. They were willing to accept the idea that because of its size or for historical reasons one clan segment could be more influential than another, and they recognized that the chiefs of such groups had the right to play a special role in the affairs of the tribe. They did not conclude, however, that this gave any chief the right to interfere in the internal affairs of a clan segment other than his own. This insistence on the right of clan segments to manage their own affairs provided each chief, however small his clan segment, with a solid and inalienable basis of power.

The power of the head chief was also limited because at least some of the other chiefs on the tribal council were recognized as being responsible for particular matters pertaining to the government of the tribe or confederacy. These charges were seen as inherent in the office itself and were passed on from generation to generation. For example, a chief named *Tsondechaouanouan* was entrusted with all matters pertaining to the tribes the Huron visited by water along the shores of Lake Huron. Messages sent from the Huron to other tribes or confederacies were usually sent in his name. A similar situation is found among the Iroquois, where particular sachems or council chiefs were held responsible for those duties that had been assigned their predecessors at the founding of the confederacy.

It appears that any chief could call a meeting about a problem falling within his own sphere of concern. Most meetings, however, were called by the tribal chief and met in the tribal capital. Some chiefs had to travel considerable distances to attend these meetings, which were held in winter as well as in summer. When a meeting was decided upon, messengers were sent out to inform the chiefs about it. Sometimes these messengers were young men, but especially if the situation was a serious one, an older man was sent, as his word would carry more weight. One of the important duties of the tribal councils was to help settle disputes between members of different villages. If the representatives of the clan segments or villages that were involved failed to mediate the dispute, the tribal council would attempt to work out a solution. The tribal council also discussed matters of interest to the confederacy as a whole with an eye to formulating proposals that would best serve the interests of the particular tribe. Often the views of the four tribes concerning foreign policy differed radically. The tribal councils, like the village councils, did not have any authority to compel tribesmen to obey their decisions; this required securing the assent of the chiefs of the clan segments, who in turn had to win the support of their followers. For this reason it is unlikely that decisions were made by majority vote, as the Jesuits state. It seems more likely that issues were discussed until a general consensus was reached. When a request was made to a council of this sort, it was usually accompanied by gifts which were put into the tribal treasury. This was used much like the stock of goods belonging to the village or the clan segments.

The Huron Confederacy

Very little is known for certain about the nature of the confederacy council or how similar it was to that of the Iroquois. It appears to have been made up of the civil chiefs who sat on the various tribal councils. Thus the chiefs who were on the confederacy council probably represented most, if not all, of the clan segments in Huronia.

An important question is the status of the Tahontaenrat, the last and probably the smallest of the tribes to join the confederacy. The Jesuits say that only three tribes were represented at the one confederacy council meeting they describe in detail. It is possible that this number is a mistake or that for some reason the Tahontaenrat were not present at this particular meeting. It may also be, however, that while the Tahontaenrat had been admitted to the confederacy about 1610, they had still not been given official seats on the confederacy council. Their position may have been similar to that of the Tuscarora who joined the Iroquois confederacy in the eighteenth century. The Tuscarora were treated exactly the same as the other tribes, except that they were not permitted to have their chiefs made official members of the council since the Iroquois were unwilling to disrupt its traditional roster of members. While the Huron were not equally inflexible in the early part of the seventeenth century, as their admission of the Ahrendarrhonon shows, it may have taken time for a small tribe, such as the Tahontaenrat, to be seated on the confederacy council. Possibly at this time they were still attending as observers.

The Jesuits suggest that the formal machinery of government on the confederacy level functioned much the same as it did on the tribal level. The two founding tribes of the confederacy were recognized as being senior to the Ahrendarrhonon and the Tahontaenrat, and the Attignawantan, by virtue of its size, seems to have dominated the Huron confederacy in a way that none of the five tribes ever dominated that of the Iroquois. The chief who presided over meetings seems to have been an Attignawantan, although he was neither of the two principal Attignawantan chiefs. In the 1630s this chief was a man who was very old and blind.

The principal meeting of the confederacy council appears to have been held each year in the spring and to have lasted several weeks. At this time new chiefs were installed and war feasts were held. There was also much singing and dancing, and presents were exchanged. The main function of these meetings appears to have been to strengthen the bonds of the confederacy by bringing together the chiefs from the various villages and providing them with an opportunity to reaffirm their friendship and discuss problems of mutual interest. Other meetings were held as issues of importance to the whole confederacy arose.

The latter meetings could apparently be called by any confederacy chief who, after consulting with his village council, decided that a matter had arisen that was important enough to deserve general consideration. He then sent out messengers requesting the other chiefs, especially those whom the matter concerned the most, to gather in his village on a particular day to discuss it. The causes for these special meetings varied. One was held during the course of an epidemic to discuss charges that the Jesuits were sorcerers who were making the Huron die. Another was called after some chiefs had slain a Frenchman who worked for the Jesuits. Disputes arising out of the murder of a member of one Huron tribe by a member of another might disrupt the league, and these were no doubt subjects for discussion by the confederacy council. If a Huron murdered a member of a friendly tribe, compensation was offered in the name of the entire confederacy, apparently by the representatives of each of the eight Huron clans. No doubt the chiefs who presented these gifts were all members of the confederacy council, and in most cases a general meeting was required to discuss what course of action was necessary. Threatened Iroquois attacks and matters of foreign policy that required quick decisions were also causes for special meetings of the council. These meetings were usually held in the house of the chief who had called them, often at night. If it was summer and greater secrecy was required, they might be held in the forest. Houses where meetings were to be held were lined with mats and fir branches for the delegates to sit on. In earlier times each chief brought his own faggots to put in the fire, but by the 1630s the women of the village tended the fires, although they did not stay for the meetings.

The Jesuits were impressed by the manner in which Huron conducted their meetings, whether at the village, tribal, or confederacy level. At meetings of the confederacy the chiefs from each village and their deputies sat together so they could consult with one another. The Attignawantan sat on one side of the council house, the remaining tribes on the other. If someone was absent, the chiefs discussed whether the meeting should begin without this person being present. Usually the decision depended on whether the items to be discussed were of particular concern to him. After this, the chiefs who had come from other villages were welcomed and thanksgiving was offered that they had arrived safely without having been attacked by enemy raiders or fallen into a stream or river. Tobacco was distributed to the more important members of the council. Then, as at the village meetings, there was a period of silence during which the counselors smoked their pipes and relaxed.

After the subject of the meeting was announced, the representatives of each tribe and village were asked their opinion on the matter and they consulted among themselves deciding what their reply would be. Then their spokesmen gave their answer, slowly and distinctly, repeating the subject under discussion and summarizing what had been said before to show that he understood it clearly. The formality of the proceedings helped to encourage politeness, moderation, and good humor, which were considered essential to the conduct of a meeting. Violent outbursts were rare and were strongly disapproved of, even if the issue was a hotly disputed one. Each speaker ended with the words "that is my thought on the subject." The assembly responded with a strong *haau*. If the person had spoken to their liking, the *haau* was given forth with much more effort. Issues often were discussed late into the night, and while the more junior members of the council might leave, the principal chiefs stayed until the end.

The language used in these councils was different from everyday speech and had a special name, *acwentonch*. Some words were used only in council speeches, and various metaphors, circumlocutions, and other rhetorical devices were employed that were not used in common discourse. Speeches were also delivered in a high-pitched and quavering voice. This made it especially difficult for the French to follow what went on at these councils.

Repression of Blood Feud

The Huron confederacy was constructed out of local clan groupings which refused to surrender any control over their internal affairs to a higher body. Action at the village, tribal, and confederacy levels required agreement among the clan segments that made up these levels, just as a chief's power to act depended upon securing the approval of his followers. Under these circumstances, the construction of the confederacy and its continued functioning were feats of no mean order. It is unlikely that without a much more complex division of labor it would have been possible for a more centralized government to have developed and gradually overridden the kin basis of Huron society. It is also quite clear that strong centrifugal forces were present which at a time of crisis or dissension could threaten the functioning and very existence of the confederacy. These forces were a source of great anxiety to the Huron, who strove to minimize their effect. Nowhere are their efforts to do this more apparent than in the sphere of law.

The Huron recognized four main classes of crime: murder and its lesser equivalents wounding and injury, theft, witchcraft, and treason. The most potentially disruptive of these was murder. Murder placed an obligation upon the kinsmen of the dead man to avenge his killing by slaying the murderer or one of his relatives. This, in turn, could lead to a prolonged blood feud between the clan segments, villages, or tribes to which the two parties belonged. Possibly, when all the peoples of the Northeast lived in small groups and depended mainly on hunting and gathering, this was the usual way of avenging murders. Bodies riddled with arrows and additional skulls, which possibly resulted from headhunting, are not uncommon in graves from the preagricultural period (Trigger 1967:156). With the development of agriculture and the growth of large villages and confederacies the effect of such disputes must have become intolerable, and new ways of dealing with murder had to be devised. The importance that the Huron placed on the suppression of blood feuds is shown by Brebeuf's comment that blood revenge was considered the most reprehensible of all crimes—far worse than murder itself.

While every effort was made to suppress blood feuds, no attempt was made to redefine the traditional rights of the groups involved. Tribes and clan segments theoretically retained the right of blood revenge, but it was agreed that in practice blood feuds within the Huron confederacy would be settled by the payment of reparations. Murder continued to be viewed as a matter concerning the respective social groups to which the murderer and his victim belonged, and society as a whole did not presume to pass judgment on any individual for the crimes he had committed. The personal treatment that he received was a matter for his own clan segment and lineage to decide. Normally, it took the form of rebukes and insults rather than any kind of physical punishment. All the members of a clan segment usually shared the cost of paying reparations for a murder committed by one of their group. They also shared in the distribution of reparation presents if a member of their segment was murdered by an outsider. If kinsmen resorted to blood revenge, not only were all their rights to receive compensation forfeited but they themselves were regarded as murderers and were required to pay the regular indemnities as well. Only if, after prolonged discussion, the clansmen of the murderer refused to pay compensation did the relatives of the murdered man have the right to take up arms against them. This happened only rarely.

It is reported that in earlier times, in addition to the fine his clan segment, village, or tribe had to pay, a murderer was compelled to lie in a cage directly under the rotting corpse of his victim until the latter's relatives gave him permission to leave. This custom was practiced nowhere in Huronia in the historic period, and possibly it belonged to a particular tribe, who had given it up after they had joined the confederacy. It may also have been a more general custom that was replaced by more elaborate compensation as the fur trade grew more important among the Huron. Even in this case, however, the family of the murdered man had to stop short of killing the murderer and thereby giving his relatives cause to avenge his death.

The exact constitutional mechanisms for settling blood feuds are unclear. It seems fairly certain that if a murder was committed within a clan segment, it was treated as a matter of concern to that group alone, although payments were probably made from one lineage to another. If a member of one clan segment killed a member of another within the same village, the settlement seems to have been arranged by the village council. If the murderer and his victim lived in different villages, the Jesuits state that the affair became a matter of concern for the two village councils. We have already suggested that in theory the dispute may have concerned only two clan segments, but that the other segments in each of the villages probably supported the parties involved, and the murderer's village may have helped his clan segment to collect the goods needed for their compensation payment. If the settlement was difficult to arrange, the affair became a matter of concern for the tribal council, which no doubt used its good offices to effect a solution. The same is true of the confederacy council, if the murderer and murdered man belonged to different tribes.

The importance of clan ties in legal settlements is indicated by the role that was played by the sisters, uncles (mother's brothers), and nephews (sister's sons) of murder victims in avenging their deaths. When the Attignawantan were struck by an epidemic after the murder of the French trader Etienne Brule, they assumed that his sister or uncle was practicing witchcraft against them. Likewise, the Jesuits speak of nephews rather than sons accusing them of witchcraft when various Huron died. Lalemant stated that a niece was a surer support for a man than were his own children. The responsibility of a clan segment to defend one of its members did not cease even if that person was married and living elsewhere. A woman's relatives are said to have been entitled to claim reparations for her murder even though she was living in another village.

The amount of compensation varied according to the rank and sex of the murdered person. If a chief or Old Man was slain, the compensation was greater than for someone of little importance, and the compensation was greater for a woman than for a man. The reasons given for the latter practice were that women were less able to defend themselves and that they were more valuable because of their reproductive capacities. The average compensation for a man was about thirty presents and for a woman forty. If the dispute were between the Huron and some other group with whom they traded, the amount was even greater; in the latter case, however, the burden on any one individual was less since the compensation was paid by the confederacy as a whole rather than by the members of a village or clan segment. Each of the reparation presents had the approximate value of a beaver robe. Those receiving compensation had the right to reject any present they believed was unworthy and to demand another in its place. After the amount of compensation was settled by the groups concerned, a bundle of sticks was presented to the murderer's tribe, village, or clan segment indicating the number of presents that were required. The chiefs divided these sticks among the various groups involved and exhorted their followers to provide the needed presents. It does not appear that the household of the murderer was asked to provide more presents than any other. Clansmen and fellow villagers often vied with one another to show their public spiritedness in helping the murderer's family.

The ceremony of presenting these presents was a formal one and often lasted several days. The presents were divided into two classes. The first were to make peace with the victim's relatives and to assuage their desire for revenge. Gifts of the second class were placed on a pole and raised above the head of the murderer. Each of these presents had its own particular name which expressed the symbolic act that it was intended to accomplish. The first two expressed the regret of the murderer and his wish to restore the dead person to life. Others were given to restore the unity of the country and to console and remove the bitterness from the hearts of the dead man's relatives. Then a series of presents was given representing things the deceased had used during his life: robe, canoe, bows, arrows, and so forth. At the end of the ceremony the relatives of the dead man gave some small presents to the group paying compensation as evidence that they were forgiven and the matter closed.

The Jesuits praised the way in which the Huron were able to prevent murders without employing the death penalty. To a seventeenth-century European it seemed almost impossible to restrain men from killing each other in the absence of capital punishment. By making tribes, villages, and especially clan segments responsible for the behavior of their members, the Huron were able to secure order within the confederacy without interfering with the traditional rights of these groups. Since all the members of a group stood to lose through the misbehavior of any one member, it was in everyone's interest to bring pressure to bear on him to behave properly. Moreover, someone who repeatedly committed crimes gradually alienated his clansmen, and there was danger that they might make reprisals against him. One woman is reported to have been killed by her brother because she was an incorrigible thief. Other individuals were expelled from their longhouses and shunned by the members of their household. If no one was willing to help such a man, he was forced to perform women's tasks and thus was made an object of public ridicule. Hence the network of social relations within each clan segment served to control its members.

In arranging for reparation payments the chiefs acted as judges or referees. One of their duties was to determine who had actually committed the murder. This was not always easy since murderers often killed their victims in the fields or while they were traveling between villages and tried to make the murder appear to have been the work of Iroquois raiders. Other murders were planned so that suspicion would fall on other Hurons. In one case, a man robbed his father-in-law and carried the loot to his mother's house in another village. In accordance with Huron custom his father-in-law went to the mother's house and carried off everything he found there. The thief then plotted to kill his own brother so that the blame for it would fall on his father-in-law and the father-in-law and his village (or clan segment) would be forced to pay compensation. After he had committed the crime, the man accused his father-in-law not only of robbery but also of murder. On the basis of his evidence, the village of the accused was compelled to pay reparations. Later a girl testified that she had witnessed the murder and the father-in-law was cleared of the accusation.

Other Crimes

Wounding was a less serious offense than murder. It was compensated with presents that varied in value according to the seriousness of the injury and the status of the person who had been attacked. There is no evidence that wounding resulting from deliberate assault was differentiated from that caused by accidents. Cases were judged by the village chiefs and the compensation was paid either by the village or the offender. If the person who was injured was of high status and from another village, he not only received compensation but a feast was given in his honor as well, while his assailant was denounced by the villagers.

The French were critical of the Huron for their stealing and the lenient attitude they took toward thieves. In their view the Huron enjoyed stealing and regarded it as an accomplishment. This seems, however, to be an unjust evaluation. Because of the communal nature of Huron dwellings and the lack of any police force, there was little that could be done to protect one's movable possessions against theft. Moreover, the Huron attitude toward property was much less possessive than that of the Europeans; hence theft was intrinsically a matter of less concern to them. The main concern of the Huron was to minimize the disruptive consequences of quarrels that might arise over accusations of theft.

One way of doing this was to define theft very narrowly. Theft was the removal of goods from an individual by force or from a cabin without permission. A person was legally entitled to claim as his own anything that he found lying about unattended. A situation described in the Jesuit *Relations* provides an interesting example of the enforcement of this rule. A poor woman temporarily left a treasured shell collar in the fields, where it was found and claimed by a neighbor. When the case was taken before the chiefs, they pronounced that the woman who had taken the necklace was legally entitled to keep it, but added that if she did not want people to think badly of her she should return it, perhaps in return for a small present. This case is an interesting example of the working of the Huron legal system because it demonstrates not only the regard that was shown for abstract rules but also how these rules could be interpreted so as to produce a socially more satisfactory solution. In order to protect their valuables, both from thieves and from fire, the Huron hid them in caches dug into the floors of their houses or else carried them around with them.

The Huron did not impose any fines or penalties on a thief personally, and they did not permit a man from whom goods had been stolen to reclaim these goods without first enquiring how a man in whose possession they were found had come by them. If the man said he had got them from someone else, he was expected to give the man's name and the owner was required to question that man in turn. A refusal to answer constituted an admission of guilt. Shamans were also sometimes hired to uncover a thief, but their methods were said to work only if the thief was present in the audience and betrayed himself by showing fear. Once a man was able to prove who had robbed him, he had the right to go with his relatives to the thief's longhouse and to carry away by force everything inside it. Thus the household of a man who had stolen very little might be despoiled of everything it possessed. Again, pressure was put on the kin group to enforce the good behavior of its members.

To prevent this rule from being used as an excuse for one extended family to rob another, it was required that an accusation of theft be supported with evidence before action could be taken. Another example of the Huron concern to prevent brawling between families and a deterioration in public order was the rule that permitted the owner of a trade route to despoil anyone using it illegally, provided that he had not yet returned to the village. Afterward there might be complaints, but no action was taken.

Two crimes were regarded as deserving punishment by death. Witches caught casting spells could be slain by anyone without fear of penalty or condemnation. Traitors, who sold information to the enemy or plotted the ruin of their people, were also killed if they became dangerous. While the latter were usually slain on the orders of a chief, in theory anyone had the right to slay a witch. Moreover, a sick man's dream, a rumor, or being seen alone in the woods was enough to arouse suspicions of witchcraft in some people's minds. In times of crisis when tensions ran high, and especially when disease threatened the village, the fear of witches reached crisis proportions. Unless it was subject to some form of social control, the right to kill witches could have degenerated into a mere excuse for killing people and could have had extremely disruptive consequences. In the next chapter how this fear was kept under control and how the chiefs were able to manipulate it as a source of power will be examined.

7

Power in Huron Society

The Ideal of Independence

WE HAVE ALREADY NOTED some strong egalitarian trends in Huron social organization. Every family was engaged in subsistence farming, and the political organization remained firmly grounded in the kinship system. Families and individuals did not seek to accumulate extraordinary amounts of property as an end in itself; instead, it was distributed in an effort to acquire social approval. In theory, and to a large degree in practice, leadership was a process that involved repeatedly securing the consent of a man's followers and thus it remained highly personal. Under these conditions it is not surprising that the Huron lay great stress on an egalitarian view of man.

Like many other traditional societies, the Huron valued conformity, so much so that a man or woman was judged very largely according to his or her ability to live up to unchanging ideas of appropriate behavior. Idiosyncratic behavior was strongly discouraged, except in a few restricted and well-defined social contexts. The Huron greatly feared dishonor and reproach; hence gossip and public criticism were strong factors making for conformity in Huron life.

However, it is a fallacy of our own culture to equate intolerance of idiosyncratic behavior with a lack of respect for the dignity of the individual. The Huron strongly objected to individuals or groups overtly trying to coerce someone to behave contrary to his own wishes. If such coercion came from outside a person's lineage or clan segment, it was an affront to the individual's clansmen as well as to himself. While an individual attempted to live up to the ideals of his society, he remained highly sensitive of his honor and personal independence in his relationship with others.

We have seen evidence of this independence in the behavior of Huron men. The ideal man was a brave warrior who was self-reliant, intolerant of restraint, and indifferent to the pain others might try to inflict on him. These values were inculcated into boys at an early age, and Huron men continued to test their courage and self-reliance throughout life. A subconscious fear of dependence on others and particularly of dependence on women may in part explain why Huron men spent so much of their lives in pursuits that took them, often for long periods of time, away from their homes and villages. This independence may also reflect the failure of Huron men to abandon attitudes that had been a vital part of life in a small hunting band in the period prior to the Hurons' growing dependence upon agriculture.

Huron culture showed equal concern for the individual dignity of women and children. Even if women did not play the important role in Huron political life that later writers claim for them, their general equality with men was noted by the French. Women freely expressed their opinions on a wide variety of topics and, especially in the home, they often behaved contrary to their husbands' wishes. Moreover, they had the same rights to divorce as men did. While women were less sensitive about their honor and tended to work together easily, an examination of legal cases and curing feasts suggests that there was no less concern for their rights and well-being as individuals than there was for those of men. The Huron refusal to use corporal punishment to train children reflects their view that the child was an individual with rights and needs of his own, as opposed to the European view of a child as an unformed being that must be molded and constrained to become an acceptable adult (Tooker 1964:124).

The right of the individual to be free from overt constraint is also evident in Huron law, where it was reinforced by the jealousy with which Huron lineages and clans guarded their privileges and independence. Huron law did not permit society as a whole to punish individuals. Even murder was punished through the payment of compensations not by the murderer but by his tribe or clan to the tribe or clan of his victim. Individuals who habitually caused trouble for their families might be subject to informal sanctions or be ostracized by them. One instance is even reported of such a person being killed. Generally, however, the assumption of responsibility for individuals by their group served to reinforce their ties with the group at precisely the same time that psychological pressures to conform were being brought to bear upon them; hence the psychologically punitive aspects of these sanctions were muted. The aim of Huron legal action was evidently not to punish the offender but to awaken in him a sense of responsibility toward those closest to him.

Suicide

Huron sensitivity concerning their honor was reflected in a high suicide rate. People are reported taking their own lives either because of excessive grief or because of humiliations they suffered at the hands of others. One man committed suicide because his wife left him, another because the losses he had incurred while gambling made him ashamed to face his relatives. Parents tended to indulge their children, fearing they would commit suicide if they were treated severely. The methods that are noted for committing suicide were eating a poisonous root, identified as water hemlock (*Cicuta maculata*),[1] or hanging oneself. Emetics appear to have been known that were used as an antidote for this poison. Prisoners who committed suicide to avoid torture were regarded as contemptible and cowardly.

Privilege

It seems fairly clear that the underlying ideals of Huron culture were egalitarian ones. At this point, however, we must inquire how perfectly these ideals were realized in Huron society. The absence of a complex division of labor that would have promoted a greater degree of social stratification and the retention of much jural and political authority within the clan segments must have helped to conserve many of the less formal egalitarian features of government that had prevailed in earlier times. However, by 1610 the Huron confederacy embraced about 20,000 people, and although built out of simple elements, the government was a complex, delicately balanced structure. The most important political offices, not only in the clan segments but also at the tribal and confederacy level, were hereditary within particular lineages, and chiefs are reported to have made their close relatives their deputies and counselors. Within each community there existed privileged families who enjoyed advantages that were denied to others. These included the chiefly lineages and the families of individuals who had acquired importance through their generosity or prowess in war. The chiefs of the village would sanction village curing ceremonies only for members of such families, judging their sickness alone to be of public importance. Likewise, these were the families that received prisoners for adoption and torture to compensate them for their losses. The existence of privileged lineages and privileged individuals suggests what we might otherwise have suspected from the size and structure of the confederacy: There were features present in it that contradicted the egalitarian ideals the Huron cherished. This discrepancy further suggests that more coercion was required to assure the operation of Huron society than can be accounted for in its overt structure. While chiefs were expected to adjudicate disputes, direct communal activities, and provide leadership in time of crisis, their ends were ideally accomplished by winning the support of public opinion. There was no constitutional means by which a chief could force his will on anyone else. To have attempted to act counter to public opinion would almost certainly have led to the repudiation of a chief by his followers.

Some of the powers and privileges of the chiefs are worth recapitulating. Chiefs were the recipients of many outward signs of respect, although there were no forms of address to distinguish them from any other older man. They were invited to many feasts, both in their own village and elsewhere, and were presented with the best servings of food that were available. We have already seen

---

[1] Also identified as Mayapple or mandrake (*Podophyllum peltatum*) (Thwaites 1896–1901, Vol. XIII:270).

that not only did the chiefs determine the number of young men that could leave the villages in the summer but some of them controlled particular trade routes as well. The permission of these chiefs was required before anyone else could legitimately trade along these routes. Presents were required to secure this permission, and the more important routes appear to have been controlled by some of the leading chiefs. No doubt, these chiefs profited from the control of these routes and were well provided with trade goods that they could distribute among their followers to validate and enhance their status.

Certain chiefs also carried on negotiations with foreign tribes, particularly tribes with whom the Huron were at war, without informing others of the nature of these discussions. Often the talks concerned the release of prisoners. Sometimes, if negotiations were desired, an important prisoner was let go free in such a way that it looked as if he had escaped. The chiefs who engaged in diplomacy of this sort seem to have been older men who were anxious to minimize conflicts. Fear of public opinion being against them appears to have made these chiefs quite secretive about their activities. The main objections to their actions were likely to have been raised by the young men, who were anxious to fight. It is likely that only the more important war chiefs knew the identity of the spies and informers that the Huron maintained among neutral and hostile tribes. These spies were probably paid out of the communal funds that were kept by the tribal and confederacy chiefs. It is unclear to what degree the chiefs were accountable to the people or to each other for the use of these funds.

Chiefs are reported to have reserved the best part of any present for themselves. Perhaps this means that they appropriated larger shares of reparation payments and other legal settlements for themselves than they passed on to their followers. No doubt, however, they also made larger contributions to these payments when these were required. The Jesuits report that the older and more important chiefs took advantage of a ritual redistribution of furs at the Feast of the Dead in order to appropriate a large number of these furs for themselves. Likewise, it is reported that when a Huron or a stranger wanted to obtain some favor, he offered bribes to the chiefs "at whose beck and call all the rest moved." Knowledge that this happened led to accusations of corruption and to jealousy and bickering among certain chiefs.

Witchcraft and Treason

There is at least some evidence that Huron chiefs and their families regarded themselves as constituting a privileged group within Huron society. This raises the further question: To what degree did the incipient class loyalties of these people covertly override their traditional loyalties to their clansmen? The answer to this question may be found by asking yet another: Granted that chiefs did act together in terms of class interests, what sources of power could they call upon to impose effective, if unconstitutional, sanctions upon their followers?

To answer this question, we must examine the two classes of individuals whose behavior was deemed sufficiently disgusting and immoral to put them beyond the pale of protection of any clansman or fellow Huron, in effect to cut them off from any normal contact with their society and to make them enemies of their own people in much the same sense that the Iroquois were. The two crimes that could do this were treason and witchcraft.

According to the Huron, certain illnesses were caused by witchcraft. Such diseases did not respond to curing by natural methods and could be detected either by a shaman or by the sick person discovering the cause of his illness in dreams. The Huron believed that the principal motivation for witchcraft was jealousy. Thus if a man had been particularly successful in trade or hunting or if a family's harvest had been particularly good, they felt in danger of witchcraft. One way to attempt to avert trouble was for a person to share the fruits of his good fortune with his neighbors. Yet even slight offenses might cause a witch to seek to do someone harm; hence even the most generous individual was in danger.

Shamans, called *ontetsans* or *aretsan*, specialized in treating diseases caused by witchcraft. The disease was assumed to be the result of the witch making a foreign object, such as a tuft of hair, nail parings, an animal's claw, a piece of leather, a pebble, or some sand, enter a person's body. It was believed that in order to do this the charm had to be rubbed with the flesh of an *angont*, a monstrous serpent that lived underground or in the water and which caused disease, death, and misfortune. The aim of the shaman was to remove this charm or at least to give the appearance of having done so. This was done by giving the patient an emetic to make him vomit, by sucking the charm from his body, or by extracting it with the point of a knife without leaving an incision. One skilled performer is said to have shaken a man who was ill with a high fever and made sand come forth from all parts of his body. Sometimes as many as twenty charms were "removed" from a sick person's body. If the person was not cured, it was assumed that still others remained concealed.

The Huron feared witches, so much so that families who felt threatened by them sometimes moved from one village to another. They were agreed that witches (*oki ontatechiata*, "those who kill by spells") should be put to death and that if they were caught performing an act of sorcery they could be slain by anyone without fear of penalty or public condemnation. In the face of strong public opinion, no one would undertake to defend a witch or to avenge their death. Formal trials on charges of witchcraft were infrequent, but from time to time people were slain as witches.

Needless to say, no one admitted to being a witch. The Huron believed, however, that clues could be found either in the dreams of sick men or in the deviant behavior of the witches themselves. Overtly antisocial activities, such as the refusal to give feasts or to be sufficiently generous with one's neighbor, might arouse suspicion. Likewise, repeated misbehavior seems to have left an individual open to an accusation of witchcraft. For the most part these suspicions did not lead to anything beyond threats and veiled accusations meant to frighten the individual and induce him to conform with social norms.

It is clear that once again Huron theory and practice cannot have been in harmony. Unless subject to some form of social control, the right to kill suspected witches without fear of punishment could have been used as an excuse for indiscriminate killings. It must be determined under what conditions an individual could be certain that society would recognize that the person he killed was a witch and also under what conditions the murdered person's kinsmen were induced to accept this verdict and to refrain from demanding compensation for the killing.

In many of the cases that are described in detail, the witches appear to have been slain on the orders of an individual chief or of a village council. Chiefs are reported threatening individuals whose behavior had elicited their disapproval (mainly the Jesuits and their converts) that they would accuse them of witchcraft and see they were killed unless they changed their ways. The threat of death was even formalized: "We will tear you out of the ground as a poisonous root." At least some accusations of witchcraft were discussed at secret meetings of chiefs. Sometimes it appears that when a person was judged guilty, the verdict was pronounced *in absentia* and an executioner was appointed to kill him without warning. Most, if not all, of the apparently spontaneous killings of witches may have been of this type.

In other instances the witch was arraigned for trial. It was once suggested to the Jesuits at a council meeting that a confession of witchcraft should be tortured from them. In another case a woman was ostensibly invited to a feast. On arrival, she was accused of witchcraft and one of the chiefs said she should be killed immediately. Then she was tortured to make her reveal her accomplices and was told to name someone to be her executioner. She was further tortured with fire outside the house and finally her head was split open and her body burned.

The association between chiefly sanction and the actual slaying of people as witches seems to be important. No doubt, in spite of the rule that said anyone could kill a witch, most people were restrained from actually doing so by fear they would be accused of having murdered an innocent person. However, as long as they agreed among themselves, the chiefs were able to sanction such killings and could use their known power to do so to frighten individuals into seeking safety in approved forms of behavior.

The Jesuits also report that many murders that were committed by the Huron were made to look like the work of Iroquois raiders. Sometimes this was done by individuals, but the chances of the deception being discovered seem to have been considerable. However, since the chiefs investigated all cases of violent death, they had it in their power to declare that murders they did not choose to investigate further had in fact been committed by the enemy. A chief who held a high office in a ritual healing society threatened to kill one of its members and make it appear to be the work of the Iroquois after the woman had converted to Christianity. Likewise, traitors are said to have been killed quickly and quietly. Possibly this was in the form of such disguised murders. The circumstantial evidence that surrounds the death of a convert who led the Jesuits into trading territory where the Huron did not wish the French to go suggests that he was killed by the order of the Huron chiefs, although his death was attributed to the Iroquois. So serious had been his offense that none of his relatives dared protest what had happened, although it seems that his brother, a fervent pagan, expressed a silent protest by converting to Christianity soon afterward.

Since the chiefs established the legitimacy of all killings of suspected witches and traitors, they were in a position to eliminate troublesome individuals and chronic offenders. This gave them a good deal of additional power to coerce individuals whose behavior tended to be radical or socially disruptive or who challenged their own authority too much. For the use of coercive power to be effective, the chiefs in any one village had to be certain that none of their number would raise a public protest concerning what they had done. Most importantly, this meant securing the consent of the chiefs who belonged to the same clan segment as their intended victim. Thus chiefs were likely to act only when they felt that their interests as a group were at stake or when they perceived the interests of the village as a whole transcending those of their own clan segment. The very fact that the latter view was possible suggests that Huron social organization was in the process of evolving away from a strictly kin base.

Thus the Huron chiefs were able to use crimes considered so heinous as to transcend all considerations of kin ties as a means of enhancing their own power as a group and of bringing pressure to bear upon individuals to behave in a socially responsible manner. At first glance, the fear of witchcraft would appear to be a socially disruptive force. In fact, by making the individual Huron highly conscious of his neighbor's potential envy, witchfear was a strong force promoting a sense of community responsibility and assuring the realization of the communal and egalitarian ideals of Huron society. Likewise, fear of treason or betrayal tended to heighten the Hurons' sense of the ties that bound them together. It is ironic that these same fears served as the basis for a *de facto* authority that was needed for the management of Huron society, but one which the emphasis on individual dignity and the rights of the Huron kin groups made ideologically unacceptable.

8

Integrative Institutions

THE HURON had a term *onderha* which meant the foundation, prop, or maintenance of a country. This term was used to refer to the dances, customs, and ceremonies that bound a people together and promoted friendship, solidarity, and goodwill among individuals regardless of their clan or lineage affiliations. The ethnographic record supports the Huron view of the importance of these observances.

Collective Beliefs

Collective activities in Huron society were based upon common beliefs. Like the activities, these beliefs tended to cut across clan and tribal boundaries. They also served to lessen the gap between the male and female spheres of Huron life. Specialized knowledge of Huron mythology and traditions was the property of certain elderly men. At feasts, these men were called upon to recite their stories. In this way the traditions of the past were transmitted to the younger generation and the solidarity of Huron society, past and present, was reaffirmed. That older men should guard and transmit this lore is in keeping with the role that the elderly played in Huron life generally. It is regrettable that so little of their lore was recorded and preserved in the seventeenth century.

The Huron believed that everything, including objects that were manmade, had a soul. The animate spirits that resided in the earth, rivers, lakes, and elsewhere in nature exerted control over trade, travel, war, disease, and other aspects of human life. These spirits possessed power to do things that an ordinary man could not do. Spirits who possessed such power were called *oki*. Human beings who possessed unusual powers or characteristics, such as shamans and witches, valiant warriors, unusually successful traders, or lunatics, were also called *oki*. Such people were believed either to possess supernatural powers or to have a particular companion spirit that endowed them with their special qualities. Charms too were called *oki*.

The most important of all spirits was the sky. It controlled the seasons, held in check the winds and waves, and assisted men in times of need. The sky was invoked whenever an important bargain or treaty was concluded and it was believed that if such an oath were broken, the sky would punish the offender. Offerings of tobacco were made to the sky, and it was thought highly improper to mock it. Prisoners appear to have been tortured and killed in its honor.

As among the neighboring Algonkian tribes, the thunder was believed to be a bird that lived in the sky. When he came to earth to feed, the flapping of his wings created the sound of thunder. In addition to exercising control over the rain, the thunderbird apparently controlled bugs and other insects, which multiplied in the dry season.

Certain large rocks were believed to be the homes of spirits. Some were located along the trade routes that were frequented by the Huron. As travelers passed by these rocks, they made offerings of tobacco to them. This was done by throwing the tobacco into the campfire or the river or else leaving it in clefts in the rock. As they did so, they would pray to the spirit of the rock to protect their homes and make their journey prosper. Even the familiar landscape of Huronia abounded with the supernatural. One evil spirit, Atechiategnon ("he who changes and disguises himself"), was associated with Tandehouaronnon, a small hill near the village of Onnentisati in the Penetanguishene Peninsula. Another spirit, associated with a large island, caused storms and fed on the corpses of those who drowned. This spirit resembled fire.

Like the other peoples of the Northeast, the Huron lacked specialists who performed regular religious ceremonies on behalf of the whole community, and they did not construct special buildings, shrines, or altars for religious purposes. Religion did not have a well-defined sphere of its own in Huron life, but tended to pervade all of their activities. The absence of specific cults may explain why, for the most part, Huron spirits tended to be only very crudely personified.

Some supernatural beings appeared in human form in dreams and visions. *Ondoutaehte,* the god of war, manifested himself either as an ugly male dwarf or as a woman. The most extensive data that have been preserved concern two of the most important and best-personified Huron supernatural beings: Iouskeha and Aataentsic.

Iouskeha, the son or grandson of Aataentsic, had charge of the living. It was he who had created the lakes and rivers by freeing the waters that had originally been confined under the armpit of a frog. He had also released the animals from a great cave in which they had been concealed and had wounded each of them in one leg so that they could be hunted more easily. The exception was the wolf, which he missed, and which remains hard to catch to this day. Iouskeha also made the corn grow and provided good weather. He had learned the secret of making fire from the great turtle (possibly his father) and had passed this knowledge on to mankind. Iouskeha grew old as men did, but never died since he was able to rejuvenate himself in old age and become again a man twenty-five or thirty years of age.

Aataentsic was the first woman to appear on earth and was the mother of mankind. Unfortunately, Aataentsic had an evil nature and spent her time trying to undo the good works that Iouskeha had done. It was she who made men die. Aataentsic brought epidemics among the Huron and their neighbors and had charge of the souls of the dead. She was normally an old woman, but had the power to turn herself into a beautiful and handsomely adorned young girl. Iouskeha and Aataentsic appear to have been identified with the sun and moon, respectively.

These two supernatural beings were believed to live very much as the Huron did. They had a bark house far from the Huron country which was surrounded by fields where they grew corn. Sometimes this cabin was associated with the villages of the dead, which were believed to be located west of Huronia. Occasionally, Hurons traveling far from home came upon the cabin of Iouskeha and Aataentsic. Aataentsic was likely to harm the visitors, although Iouskeha would attempt to save them. Iouskeha sometimes visited the Huron country. If he appeared in the cornfields carrying a well-developed stalk of corn, it signified a good harvest; if he was seen gnawing on a human leg, the crops would be bad. Iouskeha and Aataentsic also attended festivals in Huronia disguised as mortals. Iouskeha sometimes used these occasions to trick and make fun of Aataentsic.

Both of these supernatural beings played an important role in the Huron myth of creation. The Huron believed the world to be a large island supported on the back of a turtle which swam in the primeval ocean. They also believed that the earth had a hole or burrow in it into which the sun set; coming out the other end the next morning. According to one account, an eclipse of the sun occurred when the turtle shifted his position and brought his shell in front of the sun.

The Huron believed that originally Aataentsic had lived in the sky. There the spirits live much as men do on earth. One day, either when chasing a bear or cutting down a tree to obtain medicine for her husband, Aataentsic dropped through a hole in the sky and began to fall earthwards. The great turtle saw her fall and asked the other aquatic animals swimming in the primeval sea to dive to the bottom and bring up soil to pile on his back. In this way the earth was formed and Aataentsic landed gently on it.

When Aataentsic fell, she was pregnant. She became either the mother or maternal grandmother of two boys: Tawiscaron and Iouskeha. When they grew up, Iouskeha fought with Tawiscaron, who seems to have inherited many of Aataentsic's bad qualities. Tawiscaron fought with the fruits of a wild rosebush, Iouskeha with the horns of a stag. Iouskeha struck his brother so hard that the blood flowed. As he fled, the drops of his blood fell on the ground and were turned into flint (*tawiscara*), which the Indians later used to make their stone tools.

It is tempting to see in these myths a fascinating commentary on Huron social organization. The idea that Aataentsic was the ancestress of the human race and the unimportance that is attached to paternity as opposed to the mother-son relationships seem to be fairly straightforward reflections of the matrilineal bias of Huron society. However, the roles assigned to Iouskeha and Aataentsic are in many ways the direct opposite of those of men and women in everyday life. Among the Huron, men committed most of the real and symbolic acts of violence. It was they who tore down the forests, killed fish and animals, and hunted one another. Women were associated mainly with creative, life-giving pursuits. They bore children, grew crops, and attended to the care of the home. Iouskeha was portrayed as having made the world habitable and as having filled it with plants and animals that were useful to mankind. He made the crops grow and protected human beings from all kinds of malevolent influences. While he was capable of violence (he fought and wounded his twin brother), it is clear that Iouskeha was primarily associated with benevolent, creative endeavors. Far from helping to sustain life, Aataentsic sought to spoil the good that Iouskeha had accomplished. She afflicted mankind with sickness and death and sought to hurt human beings whenever she could.

It is possible that by conferring certain human characteristics on mythical figures of the opposite sex, these myths were attempts to compensate both sexes for the limitations that were inherent in the roles assigned to them in real life. Women, on the one hand, were flattered by being mythologically endowed with dangerous and aggressive qualities that they may have possessed only in men's imaginations. On the other hand, men had their real role as destroyers of life complemented by a symbolic role as sustainers of life. Iouskeha behaved entirely differently from Aataentsic, yet lived with her. Similarly, however much Huron men may have gloried in being self-reliant warriors, they remained psychologically and materially dependent on their women, and for this reason probably secretly envied them. These feelings may have been exacerbated because women's activities kept them at home and made them the focus of village life, whereas male occupations often separated them from their families and villages and took them to far-off, dangerous places. The ambivalence men felt about their role may be symbolized by Iouskeha's attack upon his brother, who seems to have shared Aataentsic's destructive and aggressive nature. It seems no accident that Tawiscaran's blood turned into flint, the stone that was used to make instruments of violence. Before too much is made of these myths, however, it must be remembered that many of their elements had a wide distribution in the Northeast, among Algonkian hunting tribes as well as the Iroquoian-speaking peoples.

Feasts

The Huron enjoyed giving and attending feasts. Generosity was an important means of winning the respect and approval of others and for this reason families worked hard growing the corn, obtaining the meat, and accumulating the presents necessary to entertain and oblige their friends and neighbors. The desire to excel at this was probably the main incentive for industry among the Huron.

Each of the Huron tribes is reported to have had its own dances, customs, and ceremonies which they had brought to Huronia with them. When refugee groups, such as the Wenro, came to live with the Huron, they communicated further innovations to their hosts. Once new customs had been introduced into

Huronia, they spread from one tribe to another. For this reason, it is impossible to treat descriptions of Huron customs as representing either a static pattern or one that was common to all four tribes.

According to the Jesuits, the Huron had four types of feasts. The largest and most magnificent were the *atouronta ochien*, or singing feasts. Often, hundreds of guests from all over Huronia attended these feasts, and kettles of food containing many deer and hundreds of large fish, as well as bear and dog meat, were prepared. Singing feasts were given if a man wished to become renowned, and thereby gain in status, at the investiture of new chiefs or before going to war. Feasts of this type appear to have been part of the annual celebrations that accompanied the meeting of the confederacy council.

The second type was the *enditeuhwa* or thanksgiving feast. The purpose of this type of feast is not entirely clear. These feasts were less elaborate than the singing feasts and appear to have been given by individuals to rejoice for special good fortune. If a man had been particularly fortunate in fishing, hunting, or trading, he gave a feast for his friends or for the whole village upon his return home. Individuals who had escaped danger or recovered from a serious illness likewise gave a feast to celebrate their good fortune. From time to time, the owner of a charm gave a feast to restore or increase its power. All of these may have been classified as *enditeuhwa*.

The final two categories of feasts were curing feasts and the *athataion*, or farewell feasts. The latter were given by a man on the point of death. Both of these were concerned with a crisis in the life of an individual. They will be described in a subsequent chapter.

When an important chief wished to give a feast, he sent out his invitations well in advance. He or his specially appointed messengers went about contacting the guests. Sometimes he issued a public announcement requesting the whole village to attend. Special invitations were sent to important chiefs in neighboring villages, and sometimes bundles of sticks were carried to each village representing the number of people who were invited. The sticks were then distributed by the chiefs among the people of the village. It was regarded as an insult for anyone who was personally invited to a feast to refuse to come, unless he had a good reason for doing so.

A person who was invited to a feast arrived wearing his finest clothing and ornaments. His hair was carefully made up and his face and body were often painted. Each guest brought with him his own plate and spoon. Singing and dancing sometimes began before the meal was served, sometimes afterward. Most of the dancing is described as taking place indoors, but it is hard to believe that some of it was not done in the open spaces within or near the village (Fig. 7). Inside the longhouse, the guests sat down on the mats and cedar boughs that were strewn on the sleeping platforms along either side. The men seated themselves at the upper end of the longhouse, the women at the lower, as the Iroquois still do today in their traditional religious observances. Only those who were invited to the feast entered the longhouse, and once the guests had arrived the doors were closed. After this, no one was supposed to enter. Failure to observe this rule was believed to bring bad luck and to affect adversely the purpose for which the feast was being given.

Fig. 7 Huron dance. Note that it is shown taking place outdoors.

The singing at feasts was led by two chiefs who stood in the midst of the dancers, each holding a tortoiseshell rattle in his hand. These chiefs sang the refrains; the dancers replied, "*Hé, Hé, Hé*," and shouted loudly at the end of each song. The latter formed an oval around these chiefs. They did not hold hands, but kept their fists closed. Women held their fists on top of each other straight out from the body; men waved their arms as if they were brandishing weapons. The dancers stamped their feet on the ground, one at a time and in tune with the song. The women shook their whole bodies and, after four or five steps, each dancer turned toward the person next to them and inclined their head. The dances were expected to be vigorous and were accompanied by appropriate facial gestures.

If the feast lasted all day, and some lasted several days, food was served both in the morning and in the afternoon. When a meal was ready, messengers went through the village or ascended the roof of a longhouse to call the people to the feast. Once they were assembled, the meal began in a formal fashion. The man giving the feast, or a person chose by him, announced *nequarre* ("the kettle has boiled"). To express their approval, all of the guests replied, "*Ho*," and struck the sleeping platforms or the ground with their fists. Then the master of the feast went through the longhouse announcing the contents of each kettle:

gagnenon youry ("there is a dog cooked"), *sconoton youry* ("there is a deer cooked"). Each person again replied, "*Ho*," and struck the ground with his fists. Then the servers went from row to row taking each person's bowl and filling it from the kettles. Some of the flesh of the larger animals was roasted, and pieces of it were passed around as well.

Guests invited to a feast were expected to eat heartily. At some feasts it was required that they eat everything in the kettles, even if they had to empty their stomachs by vomiting in order to do so. These were called "eat all" feasts, and they usually had a ritual purpose. The person giving the feast ate little or nothing at all. He spent his time smoking, singing, and entertaining his guests. Strangers and visitors from other villages were given the best food, and the heads of the animals that were cooked for the feast were presented to the most important chiefs who were in attendance.

Various dances and rites were considered appropriate to particular kinds of feasts. Often these rites were assigned a supernatural origin, knowledge of them having been revealed by some spirit. In addition to eating and dancing, feasts were often enlivened by various contests and games.

Ononharoia

The majority of Huron celebrations took place in the winter months or in the late autumn or early spring, when most of the Huron were living in their villages. During the summer the women were busy with their crops and men were away from the villages fighting, trading, or fishing. There is no evidence that the Huron celebrated the calendric feasts, such as Seed Planting, Corn Sprouting, Green Corn, Harvest, and Midwinter, that in later times were such an important feature of Iroquois culture. Fenton (1940:164) has observed that these Iroquois ceremonies, which seem to be of southeastern origin, are dominated by the idea of renewal and mainly serve to mark the annual crises in maize cultivation. Rituals that are now a part of the Iroquois Midwinter ceremonies are reported in the descriptions of Huron culture, but the context in which they appear seems to be entirely different. Tooker (1960:70,71) has suggested that since the seventeenth century, the principal emphasis in northern Iroquoian ceremonialism has shifted from shamanistic practices and curing ceremonies to the calendric rituals.[1] The principal changes seem to have been brought about by the "new religion" of Handsome Lake. The main forces promoting these developments may have been a growing emphasis on plow agriculture and the more sedentary life which resulted from acculturation.

The main Huron winter festival was called *Ononharoia* ("the upsetting of the brain"). While this festival appears to have taken place at least once a year in each major village, it does not seem to have been a strictly calendrical observance. The reason given for performing the *Ononharoia* was either that many people in the village were sick or else that some important man or woman was

---

[1] For lingusitic evidence in support of this theory see Chafe 1964.

ailing and the ceremony would help to cure them. The *Ononharoia* began in the evening with bands of people who felt ill at ease or threatened by sickness going through the village singing and shouting. These people entered all of the houses, where they proceeded to upset furnishings, break pots, and toss firebrands about. Occasionally these activities resulted in a house catching on fire. The next day they returned and announced that each of them had dreamed about something. The villagers were called upon to guess the nature of these dreams and to present each person with the object that had been revealed to him. As these people went from family to family, they were given kettles, knives, pipes, live dogs, skins, fish, tobacco, and various other kinds of presents in the hope that one of them would be the object they were seeking. Hints concerning what they wanted were given in the form of riddles. One of them would say "What I want and see is that which bears a lake in itself," by which he meant that he wanted a squash. Another might ask for "what I see in my eyes, it will be marked with various colors." By this he meant a glass trade bead, since in Huron the same word signified "eye" and "glass bead." At each hearth the dreamer recited or displayed the objects that he had already been offered in order to make it easier for the next person to guess his dream. If someone refused to give him a present, he went outside, picked up a stone, and placed it between himself and that person as a sign of reproach. When he was finally offered what he was looking for, he took it as a sign that the troubles that were threatening him had been averted. He thanked his benefactor, uttered a cry of joy, and rushed out of the house. Everyone present struck their hands on the ground and shouted "*Hé, é, é, é, é!*" to congratulate him. The *Ononharoia* usually lasted three days, at the end of which the participants went into the forest to cast out their madness. Afterward, they returned all the presents they had received from the villagers except the ones they had dreamed about.

Special feasts might be held if a village felt itself threatened with disaster. One shaman prescribed a feast in order to avert the misfortune that was augered by a lunar eclipse which had taken place in an inauspicious location in the sky. Shamans also recommended feasts as a means of averting drought or dangerous frosts. During one epidemic, large masks were erected over the cabin doors and archers made of straw were placed on the roofs of the houses in order to frighten away the demons who were causing the people to die. In seeking to avert such threats, the Huron reaffirmed their own social solidarity.

Curing Societies

The Huron had numerous formal structures that cut across clan and village lines. One such kind of institution was the curing societies, each of which performed specific rituals that were believed to cure certain kinds of disease. The Huron dreaded sickness and hence considered the activities of these societies to be very important. We have already noted that a woman was threatened with death when she refused to participate any longer in the activities of one of these societies after her conversion to Christianity.

Each of the curing societies had a leader, whose office appears to have been hereditary. Very often, these leaders seem to have been important chiefs whose ritual office complemented and strengthened their secular authority. People whom the society cured often joined, and after their death membership was passed on in their family. Thus the members of these societies were drawn from many different households and often from many villages.

We have relatively little information about the individual curing societies, but a number of dances that are described appear to have been the property of these fraternities.

One curing society was the *atirenda*. It consisted of about eighty people, including six women. This society is first reported among the eastern tribes of the confederacy and did not gain any recruits among the Attignawantan until 1636. The principal dance of this society appears to have been the *otakrendoiae*. In this dance the members of the society pretended to kill one another with charms such as bears' claws, wolves' teeth, stones, and dog sinews. As the members fell under the spell of these charms, blood poured from their mouths and nostrils as they bit themselves or was simulated with red powder. The members of this society were said to be skilled in treating ruptures, but they were also rumored to avenge insults by giving patients they did not like poison instead of medicine. One initiate was given a charm in the form of a little doll which he put in his tobacco pouch and which he claimed stirred inside it and began to order feasts and ceremonies. Parallels have been drawn between this society and the Midewiwin ceremonies found among various Algonkian tribes of the Upper Great Lakes region (Tooker 1964:99). This would not be the only ritual to have been borrowed from the northern Algonkians. If the rituals of the *atirenda* are of northern origin, they may have been introduced by way of the Ahrendar-rhonon, who seem to have been on the best terms with the northern tribes.

Another society performed the curing dance known as the *awataerohi*. It is described as the most general remedy the Huron had for sickness. The members of this society handled burning charcoal and stones that had been heated red hot. The rituals of this society were extremely dramatic. There were short periods of frenzied activity following which the members lay down and fell asleep or all of them sweated for a time under blankets. Some of the members chewed hot charcoal, and after warming their hands by blowing on them rubbed the affected parts of the patient's body. Others blew or spit hot pieces of charcoal on the person who was sick. Still others put live coals into their mouths and growled like bears in the patient's ear, while other members danced holding red hot stones in their mouths. During these dances so much burning material was scattered about the longhouse that its occupants removed everything of value for fear it would catch fire. Some members of this society found that they could not handle hot coals and only made a pretense of doing so. One man, who admitted that he had done this, said that eventually one night he dreamed that he could handle fire and heard a song that he remembered when he awoke. He sang this song at the next dance that the society performed and found that he could easily handle hot stones or plunge his bare arms into a boiling kettle.

Masked dancers are also reported to have performed rituals to drive away sickness. In one such dance, the performers appeared disguised as hunchbacks carrying sticks and wearing wooden masks. It has been suggested that this society was similar to the Iroquois False Faces, and Blau (1966) has even argued that the latter society was brought to the Iroquois by Huron refugees after 1650. His further suggestion that this society originated while the Jesuits were in Huronia remains highly speculative.

In other curing rituals women are described as walking on all fours, like animals. These women may have belonged to groups similar to the Iroquois Bear and Buffalo societies, whose members imitate the animal after which the society is named. Other dancers had sacks over their faces, or stuffed straw around their waists so that they looked like pregnant women. Fenton has compared these two groups with the Iroquois Longnose and Husk Face impersonators. Still other men attended curing feasts wearing a bearskin that covered the whole body, with the ears on top of the head and the face covered. These men acted as doorkeepers and took part in the dances only at the intervals. If a dog was to be sacrificed, one of them would carry it in, throw it on the ground several times until it was dead, and then give it to the person who would prepare it to be eaten at the end of the dance. In later times a doorkeeper was connected with the Wyandot spring ceremonial devoted to the recitations of tribal traditions. The Jesuits mention a man who was the leader of the "Dance of the Naked Ones." This was possibly the name of yet another society. The members of these curing societies were rewarded for their efforts with a feast and with presents from the sick man and his relatives.

Friendship

At least one passage in the Jesuit *Relations* suggests that the Huron had ritual friendships (Tooker 1964:89). Such a friendship was a formal, lifelong relationship between two people that entailed certain specific rights and obligations. Relationships of this sort are attested to among the Iroquois and also, apparently, among the Wyandot. Lalemant describes a woman being commanded in a dream to become the friend of another woman. To accomplish this she gave the woman a dog, a blanket, and a load of wood and finally invited her and her husband to a feast. The feast may possibly have been given to formalize the friendship.

A less formal social activity that brought men together was the sweat bath. Men sweated to keep healthy and to prevent disease. When a man wished to sweat, he invited his friends to join him. Sweating was done inside a small, circular hut that was heated by placing hot stones in the center of it. Because sweathouses were relatively easy to construct, they were erected not only in the villages but also in overnight camps while travelling. The men huddled closely together inside the hut, their knees raised to their stomachs. Then someone outside covered the hut with skins and pieces of bark so that no heat could escape. To encourage sweating one of the men inside the hut sang, while the rest shouted continuously as they did in their dances. They also drank large potfuls of cold water and sometimes burned tobacco. When the sweating was over, they bathed themselves in a river or washed in cold water. Sometimes, when a sick man sweated in the hope of being cured, a shaman would join the group.

Games

Games were an extremely important means of promoting social inter-action, especially between men from different villages. Sometimes games were played among individuals from the same village, but not infrequently teams from different villages played against one another. These games generated great interest and provided the people from these villages with an opportunity to get together in friendly rivalry and to enjoy each other's company. The Huron were avid gamblers and no game, however informal, was unaccompanied by a wager. Thus the games also provided an opportunity for the redistribution of goods among the Huron. The stakes in these games often ran high. One village lost thirty wampum collars in a single match, and some individuals gambled away even the clothes they wore. One person, having gambled away all he owned, staked his hair and when he lost, cut it off without any sign of regret. Another man gambled his little finger and on losing cut it off. At one point in the Jesuit *Relations* it is stated that gambling was a frequent cause of fights and murders, but this seems to be an error. Elsewhere it is stated that men and women who had lost everything returned home as cheerful and happy as if they had lost nothing. This latter sort of attitude was obviously in the spirit of Huron culture and in keeping with Huron attitudes toward property. Some individuals were sufficiently ashamed of their losses, however, that they committed suicide rather than returning home to face their families.

The three most common games that the Huron played were lacrosse, the dish game, and *aescara*, a game played with straws. These games were played by most of the tribes living around the Great Lakes. Games were often played to cure the sick or to avert disaster. Lacrosse is reported as being played to avert misfortune, stop an epidemic, influence the weather, and to honor the memory of a dead player.

Lacrosse was played with a ball and stick in a field outside the village. It was a dangerous game played mostly by young men. Injuries appear to have been not infrequent. The dish game was played with five or six fruit stones or small pottery disks painted black on one side and yellow or white on the other. In an ordinary game the players seated themselves in a circle and each one in turn placed the stones in a wooden bowl and struck it sharply on the ground. One side scored when all of the stones fell out either one color or the other. Women sometimes played with the dice, but they did not use the bowl. They took the dice in their hands and threw them into the air, letting them fall on a skin or hide stretched on the ground. Occasionally, the men and boys amused themselves by playing this game with the women. Even in these family games, however, collars, earrings, and other possessions were wagered. The third game, *aescara*, was played with three- or four-hundred white rushes, each about a foot long. The rules governing this game are unknown.

In one instance, a prominent individual asked the chiefs of his village to have the bowl game played for his health. The chiefs agreed and held a council to fix the time of the game and to decide what village should be challenged to play. When the challenge was accepted, preparations for the game began in both villages. The men who were to be on each team fasted and abstained from sexual intercourse, as they did on any occasion when they were seeking supernatural powers. Then they assembled at night for a feast, during which they performed sleight-of-hand tricks with the playing stones and resorted to divination to predict the outcome of the game. They also brought out their personal charms and exhorted them to bring them good luck. After this, they slept in hopes of having a favorable dream or one in which still further charms would be revealed.

In the morning they related their dreams and collected all the items they believed would bring them good luck. On the day of the game the teams and spectators from the two villages arranged themselves on opposite sides of a large longhouse, completely filling it. The sick man, for whom the game was being played, was brought in and the two players who were to start the game took their positions in the middle of the longhouse. When the bets between individuals on both sides had been arranged, the game began. All of the spectators shouted and gestured either to attract luck for their player or to drive misfortune to the other side of the house. Each side appears to have had a man who kept track of points lost and won. A player who was unlucky was soon replaced by another. Such a game might continue for several days, with food and hospitality being extended to all who attended.

Feasts, dances, and games were, as the Huron said, the prop of their society. These activities crosscut lineages and clan segments and brought together the people of different villages in celebrations and friendly rivalry. In the next chapter the most solemn and far-reaching of all the Huron efforts for promoting social solidarity, the Feast of the Dead, will be examined.

9

The Dead

THE HURON, like most North American Indians, did not practice any sort of ancestral cult, and they did not look to the dead for favors and support (Tooker 1968:14). The absence of ancestral cults seems correlated with a general lack of concern with precise genealogies, the strong sense of history that creates an interest in such matters being completely foreign to the Huron. Nevertheless, the most distinctive Huron customs were those associated with the burial of the dead. In this, they were heirs of a longstanding tradition among the peoples of the Northeast.

The periodic reburial of the dead in large bone pits or ossuaries, which was of such importance in Huron culture, was an Ontario Iroquoian custom not shared by the inhabitants of New York State. This custom seems to be foreshadowed in the single or multiple (perhaps family) bundle burials that were made in and around villages in Ontario in early Iroquoian times (Wright 1966: 99). In the fourteenth century small ossuaries began to be constructed close to villages. Each of these apparently contains the dead of a particular village during its ten or fifteen years of existence. Later, the Huron ossuaries grew larger as their villages increased in size and tribal entities began to play a more important role in Huron life. By the historic period, the Feast of the Dead, of which ossuary burial was the central feature, had become the most important of all rituals for binding together different Huron groups and cementing relations between the Huron and their northern trading partners. The Neutral also had ossuary burial, but their bone pits contained fewer bodies and were constructed differently from those of the Huron (Ridley 1961). The Neutrals' ceremonies for the dead were also considerably different from those of the Huron.

Death was a source of great anxiety in Huron culture. This was in part because it was conceived of as cutting a person off from effective personal contact with those he loved. The memory of the dead was cherished, but, possibly because the dead were believed to resent being severed from the community they had known, their souls tended to be feared. It was a grievous injury to remind a man of anyone in his family who had died. Simply to say "your dead relatives" was a violent curse capable of bringing people to blows. To mention a man's name without adding an honorific to indicate that he was dead was a severe insult. This is one of the reasons why chiefs quickly announced the death of an individual throughout the village. If anyone living in the village had the same name as the dead man, he changed it for a time in order not to offend the relatives of the deceased. At the same time great respect was shown for the remains of the dead. If a fire broke out in a village, the first efforts were directed toward saving the cemetery.

Beliefs about the Dead

As is in many cultures, there appears to have been considerable variation in Huron beliefs about souls and the afterlife. Human beings, as well as animals and what we would regard as inanimate objects, were believed to have souls. These souls were as large as the body they animated and had the same shape. Human souls had several parts, each corresponding to some aspect of behavior such as being active, having knowledge, exercising judgment, or desiring things. Each of these aspects of the soul had its own name.

When the corpse was taken to the cemetery, its soul was believed to walk ahead of it and to remain near the body until the Feast of the Dead. At night, these souls wandered through the village, entering houses and eating what was left of the evening meal. Some Hurons did not eat food that had been left standing over night for fear they would die if they consumed the food of the dead.

Most Huron believed that they had two souls. One remained with the body after the Feast of the Dead and did not leave it unless it was reborn as a child. According to the Huron, such acts of reincarnation explained why some children resembled their dead ancestors. Because of their belief in this soul, the bones of the dead were called *atisken*, "the souls." The other soul left the body at the Feast of the Dead and traveled to a village of the dead located in the west. Each Huron tribe or major village was believed to have its counterpart in the land of the dead. There also lived Aataentsic and Iouskeha. Some said that these souls became birds, others that they traveled west along the Milky Way, which was called *atiskein andahatey*, "the path of souls." Certain stars near the Milky Way were called *gagnenon andahatey*, "the path of dogs," and were the route by which the souls of dogs traveled westward. Still others identified the route to the afterlife with the trail leading westward to the Tionontati country. This road went past a tall standing rock called *Ecaregniondi*, which was said to be daubed with the paint the spirits used on their faces. Further along this road, the souls of the dead encountered other obstacles of Indian folklore. At one point they came across the house of the mythical *Oscotarach* (Pierce-head). He drew the brains out of the heads of the dead and kept them. There was also a river that had only one bridge across it in the form of a tree trunk. This bridge was guarded by a dog that jumped at souls and made many of them fall into the river and drown. In the villages of the dead, life was much the same as it had been on earth. The souls tilled the soil, went hunting and fishing, and participated in feasts and dances. The souls of food or utensils that the living buried with the dead were used by them in the afterlife. In spite of these similarities to the land of the living, the souls of the dead were not happy and are said to have complained day and night.

Not every soul, however, was believed to travel westward to the villages of the dead. Because they lacked the strength for the journey, the souls of old people and children remained in Huronia, where they had their own villages. They sowed corn in the fields the living had abandoned, and if a village caught fire, collected the burned corn for their own use. These souls were heard by the living from time to time. The body of a baby only a month or two old was buried under a path so that its soul might enter the womb of a woman who was passing by and be reborn. The Huron also believed that the souls of those who had died violent deaths were dangerous, and for this reason they were excluded from the ordinary villages of the dead. The souls of those who had died in battle formed a band by themselves, dreaded by their fellow Huron. Suicides were likewise excluded from the villages of the dead.

The bodies of those who died violent deaths were immediately buried or burned, and they were not dug up and reburied at the Feast of the Dead. The bones of captives, of course, found their way into the village middens, and the corpse of at least one woman slain on charges of witchcraft was publicly burned. The body of a person who had drowned or frozen to death was taken to the village cemeteries and laid on a mat. A ditch was dug on one side of the body and a fire was lighted on the other. Then some young men, chosen by relatives of the deceased, cut up the body and threw the flesh and entrails into the fire, while the skeleton was placed in the ditch. This ritual was performed to appease the sky or the spirit of the lake, who was believed to be angry. Failure to do so would result in dangerous changes in the weather and in accidents. Thus the men who cut up the body were rewarded for having performed a generous and public-spirited act. If a Huron died outside of Huronia, his body was burned and the bones extracted to take back to his native village.

The Huron claimed knowledge of the hereafter from souls who had visited them in dreams or from the visits that the souls of the living had made to the land of the dead. One Huron tale resembles the Greek myth of Orpheus, but has a distinctively Huron flavor. It tells of a Huron who, after many adventures, brought the soul of his favorite sister (not his wife) back from the realm of the dead, having struggled with it all night in order to make it small enough to fit into a pumpkin. His host in the land of the dead had told him that he could restore his sister to life by making her soul reenter her body, but warned him that he should allow no one who had to be present to watch what he was doing. When the man returned to his village, he made a feast as his ghostly adviser had counseled, but as he was attempting to resuscitate his sister, someone raised his eyes and her soul escaped.

Death and Burial of Individuals

A Huron was expected to die as bravely as he had lived. A dying man was often shown the clothing in which he was to be buried and frequently was dressed for burial before he died. A man about to die usually gave a farewell feast for his relatives and friends during which, if he were able, he partook of the best food and sang his war song to show that he did not dread death. We have already noted that these feasts were given in honor of prisoners who were about to be slain. The villagers vied with each other to present a dying man with anything he requested, believing that any frustration of his desires was a threat to his life. Death was frequently attributed to failure to provide for the wishes of a person's soul. If a man who was believed on the point of death recovered, the last present that had been given him was credited with saving his life and was treasured by him as long as he lived.

As soon as a man died, his body was flexed in a crouching position, wrapped tightly in his finest robe, and laid on the mat on which he had died. Among some of the Huron tribes, the friends and relatives of the deceased painted their faces black and also painted the face of the deceased and embellished him with ornaments and feathers. The Jesuits report that every family had someone who took charge of its dead. It is likely that particular families belonging to different clans (or phratries?) were responsible for attending to the details of each other's funerals. This not only created another bond of reciprocity within Huron society but it also freed the relatives of the deceased from having to attend to funeral arrangements during their period of mourning.

As soon as he was informed of the death, a chief or his assistant went through the village announcing who had died and urging each family to prepare some food and distribute it among the friends and relatives of the deceased. When the food was prepared, the villagers converged on the longhouse of the dead man for a wakelike observance called the *agochin atiskein*, or "feast of souls." During this observance, the women and girls of the village wept in a highly stylized manner, making their voices tremble in one accord. Each woman inflamed her own grief by reciting the names of all her relatives who had died. Their wailing and tears continued until ordered to stop by a person of authority. During this time the men did not weep, but assumed a melancholy expression, their heads sunk on their knees. Frequently, someone of importance spoke to console the relatives of the dead man, pointing out the inevitability of death and praising his good nature, generosity, and bravery.

Burial usually took place on the third day after death. This gave relatives and friends in other villages time to arrive for the funeral. If the deceased had been a person of importance, not only large numbers of friends but also important chiefs from other villages would assemble, each bearing presents in his honor. The funeral began at daybreak with a meal. This was provided to feed the guests who had arrived from elsewhere, to nourish the soul of the dead man, and as a further expression of the grief and consolation of the community.

When all the kettles were emptied, those attending the funeral assembled inside the house of the dead man and mourning resumed. The body was then covered with a beaver robe and four men carried it on a mat to the cemetery, the whole village following in silence. There a tomb had been prepared. At least among the Attignawantan, most of these tombs consisted of a bark coffin supported on four posts 8–10 feet high and sparsely painted (Fig. 8). In some villages a few corpses were buried in the ground, a bark hut or shrine was built over the grave, and a stake fence was erected to keep out dogs and wild animals. No reason is given for constructing the latter tombs, but they may have been erected over the bodies of those who had died violent deaths.

When everyone had arrived in the cemetery, an official publicly announced the presents that had been given to dry the tears of the widow and the other relatives of the deceased. These presents were then distributed among the relatives and those who had taken charge of the funeral. Only an occasional wampum collar, a comb, a gourd full of oil, or a few loaves of bread were placed in the coffin with the deceased. At some funerals, when the coffin was closed, two sticks were thrown from the top of the tomb to the young men and women who had gathered on either side. A fierce struggle ensued, the aim of which was for one person to secure possession of the stick and win a prize. When the interment was over, everyone departed quietly for home.

For ten days after the funeral the husband or wife of the deceased lay on a mat, covered with furs and with his or her face pressed against the ground. During this period, such mourners did not speak, except to say good-day to visitors. They did not warm themselves by the fire and only left the house at night to go to the toilet. Widows did not comb their hair or clean themselves during this period.

This initial period of deep mourning was followed by a year in which remarriage did not take place. During this period, widows and widowers did not grease their hair and avoided friends and going to feasts. Women went to far greater extremes in observing this period than men did. They frequently blackened their faces and went about ill-clad, unkempt, and with their heads lowered. They also frequently visited the cemetery to mourn. In some cases, however, a woman's mother might order her to cease her grief and resume a normal life before the year was ended.

Deaths also imposed restrictions on the friends of the deceased. Men usually did not go fishing after a friend had died, as the fish were believed to dislike the dead. Feasts were given in memory of the dead from time to time throughout the village. At least some of these were concerned with conferring the name or title of the deceased upon his successor.

The Feast of the Dead

The bodies of those who had not died violent deaths did not remain in the village cemeteries, but were removed from their coffins and reburied in a common bone pit at the Feast of the Dead, an observance that the Huron

Fig. 8 A Huron cemetery.

generally referred to as "the kettle." This ceremony was held at about ten- or twelve-year intervals.

There have been differing opinions concerning the nature of this feast. The sources indicate that it was planned by the chiefs of an entire tribe and that at least the Attignawantan sought to make of it a tribal festival. Brebeuf suggests, however, that the feast was observed every time a large village changed location. The number of ossuaries in Huronia that contain trade goods, and thus probably date after 1600, indicates that each of the four tribes must have celebrated more than one Feast of the Dead, if these ceremonies were observed at intervals of ten years or more. Moreover, even the largest ossuaries contain the bones of only about 1000 individuals which, assuming a normal death rate of about 2.7 people per hundred each year, would indicate a population of 3000–4000 people. This is a number too large for a single village, but too small for a tribe as numerous as the Attignawantan. Moreover, the Jesuits report that in

1636 the Attignawantan celebrated two Feasts of the Dead, one in the northern part of the country, another in the south.

The solution seems to be that a Feast of the Dead was held each time a large village changed location, and that into the ossuary were placed the dead of that village and of any satellite villages that were dependent on it. We are told that neighboring villages and tribes were notified about the feast so that those who wished that particular town to be the final burying place of their relatives might bring them there. Some of the bodies brought from a distance may have been those of natives of the village who had married outsiders. Apparently, the desire of friends to be buried together also led people to request burial in an ossuary other than that of their own village. The significance of this mingling of the dead from many parts of Huronia in the ossuary of a single village cannot be overstressed. The Huron said that because the bones of their relatives and friends were united in the same place, they themselves felt obliged to live in unity and concord. Friendly tribes from outside the confederacy were also invited to the ceremony; thus, it tended to reinforce ties not only among the Huron but also between the Huron and their allies. It is unclear to what degree tribes outside the confederacy were encouraged to bury the bodies of a few of their members in Huron ossuaries as a token of good will. The Attignawantan sought permission from the Jesuits to reinter the bodies of two Frenchmen who had died in Huronia. On the other hand, the haughty boast of this tribe that the souls of Algonkians would not be welcomed in their villages of the dead suggests that they did not permit the bones of these tribes to be buried alongside their own. It is possible, however, that the Ahrendarrhonon, who were more friendly with the Algonkians, were not so exclusive.

The Feast of the Dead lasted ten days. The first eight days were spent preparing the bodies for reburial and assembling the participants, many of whom had to come from a distance. In each village where there were individuals who planned to participate in the feast, the people went to the cemeteries, and those who had taken charge of burying a particular body removed it from its tomb, while the relatives mourned as they had on the day of burial. Only the bodies of those who had died recently were left intact. The rest were stripped of any remaining flesh and skin, which, along with the robes and mats in which they had been buried, were burned. This work was performed by the female relatives of the deceased, who are reported to have done it without manifesting any overt repugnance, although the corpses often were swarming with worms and smelled badly.

After the bones had been cleaned and washed, they were wrapped in fine new beaver skins. The relatives of the deceased often kept skins specially for this purpose, even if it meant depriving themselves of skins needed for clothing. Relatives and friends contributed beads and necklaces to the bundle so formed, saying, "I am giving this for the bones of my father [mother, or whatever relative it was]." The bundle was then put into a bag, decorated with necklaces, bracelets, and other ornaments, which a woman was able to carry on her back. Some of these bags were fashioned roughly to resemble a man sitting in a crouching position. The whole bodies were wrapped in new skins and each was placed on a litter.

Then all of the remains of the dead were taken back to the village, where each family had a feast in honor of its own. At this time, presents of skins, trade goods, and food were made to honor the deceased, and these things were displayed in the house where the parcel containing his bones was kept. In some villages, a day or two before setting out for the Feast of the Dead, all the bones were brought to the house of an important chief, who offered a magnificent feast in honor of his predecessor or someone else of note. The presents that the relatives brought were displayed on poles along both sides of the longhouse and all the guests shared their food with one another. At the end of this feast the people imitated the cry of souls and left the house shouting, "*Haéé, haéé!*"

After this, those who wished to attend the Feast of the Dead set out for the village where it was being held. The women carried the bones of the dead in the parcels in which they had been wrapped. As the procession made its way along, the women repeated the cry of souls, saying that if they did not, the burden of the dead would weigh heavily on their backs and cause them to suffer from backaches for the rest of their lives. The procession moved slowly, stopping at each village along the way. As it approached these villages, presents were exchanged and each person went to the house of a relative, or clansman, while the chiefs discussed how long the visitors should remain in the village. In this way new friendships were made and old ones reaffirmed throughout the country.

In the village where the main ceremonies were to be held, the first seven or eight days were spent preparing the bodies from the village cemetery and welcoming the guests who were arriving from other villages. These were assigned hosts, in whose cabins they placed the bones of their dead and the gifts that accompanied them. There was continual feasting and dancing, and games were played, for which prizes were offered in the name of the dead. Women shot with a bow for prizes such as a porcupine quill collar or a string of wampum, and young men shot at sticks to win beaver pelts. Meanwhile, in an open field not far from the village, a pit was dug about 10 feet deep and 15 feet or more in diameter. Around the pit, a carefully made scaffold or platform was erected up to 50 feet across and 10 feet high and ladders were put up all around it. Cross poles were erected on top of the platform to which the parcels containing the bones of the dead were later affixed. The day preceding the start of the final interment, the undecomposed bodies were brought to the edge of the pit. They were placed underneath the scaffold on mats or slabs of bark fastened to stakes 5 feet or more in height.

On the last day before the reburial of the dead, the packages containing their bones were taken down and opened so that their relatives might mourn over them again and wish them a final farewell. When the bundles were re-wrapped, a few additional presents were occasionally added to them. One woman, for example, who was the daughter of an influential chief, placed his council sticks inside his bundle.

In the afternoon all of the people went to the field where the ossuary had been dug and arranged themselves there according to villages and clan segments (Fig. 9). Each group then laid its parcels on the ground and, unfolding

Fig. 9 A somewhat fanciful drawing of the Feast of the Dead, apparently made about 1724.

the presents that had been brought in honor of the dead, hung them on poles where they remained on view for about two hours. The Jesuits noted that at the Feast of the Dead held in Ossossane in 1636, over 1200 presents were on view, most of them beaver robes. This display of presents permitted non-Huron who were attending the feast to view the wealth of the country and gave each clan segment an opportunity to display its affluence and piety toward its dead. Brebeuf noted that less affluent Huron deprived themselves of goods that they needed in order not to appear less generous or well-off than their neighbors.

In the middle of the afternoon each of the chiefs, on receiving orders from the man who was in charge of the feast, gave a signal and all of his followers, loaded with their parcels of bones, ascended the platform and hung them on the cross poles. Again, each village placed its bones in its own section.

After that, the ladders were taken away, but a few chiefs remained on the platform; it was their duty to announce the presents that were made in the name of the dead to specified persons. In this manner, many of the presents that had been put on display were redistributed by the relatives of the deceased to other persons. It is not stated to whom these presents were given, but it is possible that they went to friends of the family or to those who had performed services for them, either by acting as hosts at the Feast of the Dead or by being the people who were in charge of family burials. The formal announcement of these presents made it clear to everyone that each family had discharged its duty in this respect.

Toward evening about fifty beaver robes, each consisting of ten skins, were taken from among the presents that had been displayed, and these were used to line the burial pit.[1] This was done in such a way that the robes extended more than a foot out of the pit all around. Then some old and broken kettles and other objects were put in the bottom of the pit, for the use of the souls, and the half-decayed, but entire, bodies of the dead were lowered into the pit and arranged on the bottom. Besides the robe in which each of these bodies was wrapped, it was supplied with one, or even two, more to cover it.

All of the participants spent the night around the pit, lighting their fires and cooking their food on the spot. Normally, the bones of the dead were emptied into the pit at sunrise, unless a package of bones accidentally fell into the pit. This was interpreted as a sign that the souls wished to be interred beforehand. At a given signal the crowd again mounted the platform and each person emptied his own package into the pit, keeping, however, the robes in which the bones were enveloped. The grave goods that had been placed in the package with the bones were also thrown into the pit. At the same time, the crowd raised a great cry of lamentation. It was the duty of five or six men, stationed in the pit, to arrange the bones. This was done with poles, and the effect of it was to mingle the bones of different individuals together into a homogeneous mass.

When the pit was filled to within about 2 feet of the top, the robes bordering the edge were turned back and the space in the center was covered with mats and bark. The mourners then piled sand and wooden poles over the pit. The poles were probably those that had been used to construct the platform, and the reason for doing this was probably to prevent animals from burrowing into the pit. Some women brought dishes of corn and threw them on top of the pit to provide food for the souls of the dead. On that day and days following, several chiefs from the village where the feast was being celebrated made similar offerings to the dead.

The rest of the morning was spent distributing presents. Most of the robes in which the dead had been wrapped were sliced apart and the beaver skins that composed them were thrown from the platform into the midst of the crowd, who competed to get hold of them. When more than one person claimed the same skin, it was often cut into several pieces. Twenty robes were given to

---

[1] It is possible that one robe was donated by each of the clan segments that made up the Huron confederacy.

the chief in charge of the feast, who used them to thank the chiefs of the other tribes who were present. Others were distributed by the chiefs of the clan segments to people whom the relatives of the deceased had designated. Still others, that had been used only for show, were taken away by the same people who had brought them. The Jesuits noted that the chiefs received a large share of these presents. Some of them were probably given in recognition of their office and the services they had rendered the relatives of the deceased.

Once the pit was filled in, wooden stakes were driven into the ground all around it and a cover was erected on top. This hut or shrine, which was not replaced after the original one had rotted away, resembles those said to have been placed over certain graves in the village cemeteries. If we are correct in our suggestion that the latter were erected over the graves of those who were not intended to be reburied, it is likely that these huts were the sign of a final burial.

When this was finished, the participants feasted once again and those who had come from elsewhere took their leave to return home. Everyone is reported to have been joyous at this time and pleased that their relatives and friends had received a fitting burial and had been honored with so many presents. Much of the joy must have come from the renewal of old friendships and the reaffirmation of the ties binding the Huron peoples together. The solidarity of the participants was the greater because in one way or another everyone had been involved in the giving and receiving of presents. It would be a mistake, however, to stress the economic aspects of this ritual at the expense of other features. The great affection and concern that the Huron felt for the remains of their dead is not a negligible factor, and this concern was one that came to be shared by some of the northern tribes with whom the Huron interacted. By joining in a common tribute to the dead, whose memory each family loved and honored, the Huron were exercising a powerful force for promoting goodwill among the disparate segments of each village and tribe and of the confederacy as a whole. As the Huron trading network expanded, the Feast of the Dead was extended to promote solidarity between the Huron and their allies, although the subsistence patterns and culture of many of the latter differed radically from their own. It is little wonder that during the seventeenth century this feast was adopted, albeit in an altered form, by the Nipissings and other northern tribes as a means of promoting political and commercial relations among themselves in the early days of the fur trade (Hickerson 1960). The last Feast of the Dead in which Huron are reported to have participated seems to have been a joint Wyandot-Ottawa ceremony held at Mackinac in 1695 (Kinietz 1940:117). The Huron who were present at this feast had by now become fused with the Tionontati, and the ceremony itself probably conformed to the Algonkian rather than to the ancient Huron pattern.

10

The Individual and Society

Theories about Illness

DURING THEIR STAY IN HURONIA, Fathers Lalemant and Ragueneau recorded a great deal of information about the Hurons' interest in averting illness and healing the sick. We have already noted in passing that many rituals and community activities were concerned with invoking supernatural aid for these purposes. A comparison with other northern Iroquoian cultures suggests that this concern was not simply the result of the epidemics that were then ravaging Huronia; rather it was an important and long-standing focus of Huron culture. If Huron methods of combating physical illnesses seem primitive, their overall view of sickness and health was considerably more sophisticated.

The Huron did not limit the concept of health to physical well-being, nor was any attempt made to view the individual independently of his social environment. The Huron drew no clear line between physical and mental states, nor did they attempt to distinguish between what happened to a person as the result of his own actions and events that we would regard as accidents. The concept of health included an individual's happiness and personal fulfilment, as well as his good or bad fortune. It was thus a concept that embraced everything that affected a human being's life and self-image.

The Huron recognized three major causes of illness and disequilibrium: (1) natural causes, (2) witchcraft, and (3) the unfulfilled desires of a person's soul. The latter were called *Ondinnock*.

Natural illnesses were those that the Huron were able to treat successfully by natural means. The Huron knew of a number of herbs and drugs, although in the opinion of the Jesuits their knowledge of medicinal plants was limited. One herb they valued highly was *oscar*, perhaps wild sarsaparilla (*Aralia nudicalis*). It was used to heal wounds, ulcers, and open sores. *Ooxrat* or the root of Indian turnip (*Arisaema triphyllum*) was used to clear phlegm from the heads of old people and to improve the complexion. The root first had to be cooked in hot ashes to remove its stinging properties. Various other roots and bark were probably used by the Huron, although they are not mentioned in our sources.

The Huron also used emetics and made incisions to drain swellings. Poultices were sometimes prescribed, and sweating was considered to be good for some ailments. Injuries such as wounds caused by arrows or animal bites were also treated by natural means, although spells frequently accompanied the cures. If treatment did not succeed, it was concluded that in spite of appearances the source of the problem was either witchcraft or soul desires.

Desires of the Soul

According to Huron belief the health and fortune of an individual could be threatened both by other members of the community and by himself. The theory of witchcraft assumed that diseases, as well as other misfortunes, were caused by spells that someone had cast upon the sick man. The cure for such diseases lay in extracting the spells that had been injected into his body. We have already discussed how cures of this sort were believed to be accomplished.

In addition, every Huron was believed to have a soul that was possessed of concealed but very powerful desires. Sometimes these desires were revealed to an individual in the form of dreams, which were believed to be the language of the soul. Dreams were all the more real to the Huron because they believed that in sleep the soul issued forth from the body and proceeded to the place where the things being dreamed about actually existed. Even very young children had such desires, which occasionally were communicated to their parents in dreams. If these desires remained unfulfilled, the soul became angry and would cause its owner to suffer illness and misfortune. Once a desire had been fulfilled, a person was expected to recover rapidly.

Sometimes the desire was for a particular object, such as a canoe, a wampum collar, a dog, or for some particular kind of food. Desires of this sort played an important role in the *Ononharoia*. Other dreams gave promise of victory or warnings of danger which could be realized or averted only if certain desires of the soul were gratified. Still other dreams expressed the wish for socially unsanctioned forms of sexual gratification. An older man might wish to have a younger girl given to him for a short time so that he could have sexual intercourse with her, or he might want to watch other people performing the sexual act. Such wishes are of particular note inasmuch as the Huron were normally reluctant to express their sexual interests so publicly. Another sort of dream wish that ran counter to the norms of Huron society was that which gave expression to the hostility of one person toward another. In these dreams, the dreamer was commanded to humiliate, harm, or even kill someone else. A final class of dreams was perhaps not strictly classified as the expression of soul desires, but was intimately concerned with the inner state of individuals. These dreams involved visits of the soul or of guardian spirits to an individual who promised to confer special powers upon him if he would perform certain rites or offer them special presents. Often these presents had to be obtained from other people in the community. People who had such dreams often gave feasts to compel the soul to keep its word and to make it fulfill its promises as quickly as possible.

Wallace (1958) has noted that the majority of men's dreams fall into three classes. The first are associated with puberty and the achieving of adult status, the second with war, and the third with the fear of old age and death. Champlain and Sagard agree that women dreamed more often than men did. Often these dreams were about the death of relatives and other imaginary terrors. Visitation dreams were common to both sexes. These served to resolve some of the inner doubts and conflicts of the dreamer and permitted him to assume a new identity more in keeping with the role he desired for himself within the community.

Shamans

Although the Huron believed that their unfulfilled desires might reveal themselves in dreams, they were not always certain that their dreams had revealed the truth to them. Sometimes dreams were forgotten or a man failed to see the real significance of his dreams. In order to interpret them properly, the aid of a specialist was required.

The Huron recognized four kinds of shamans: those who were able to control the wind and rain, those who could predict future events, those who could find lost objects, and, finally, those who could heal the sick. Of these, the last were the most important. Only men appear to have served as curers; women who claimed supernatural powers restricted themselves to various forms of divination.

The general term for shamans was *arendiwane*, meaning "his supernatural power is great." *Arendiwane* who specialized in diagnosing ailments were called *ocata* or *saokata*. These men diagnosed and recommended treatment for all kinds of diseases. Each of them had an *oki* or familiar spirit who revealed to him the cause of the illness. Often this was done through dreams or visions that came immediately after awakening. On still other occasions the *ocata* determined the hidden desires of a man by gazing into a bowl of water until the desire appeared to them. Others preferred to look into fire, while still others went into a frenzy, fasted, or secluded themselves in the darkness of a sweathouse. Sometimes a medicine man would sweat with ten or twenty men in order to determine the nature of his patient's ailment. These shamans were believed to be able to penetrate into the depths of their patient's souls and to perceive their true desires, even those of children and ones which had been forgotten. The man who accompanied the *ocata* carrying his drugs and tortoiseshell rattle and who specialized in extracting spells was called an *ontetsans* or *aretsan*. Both kinds of medicine men were highly honored and esteemed and were well paid for their services.

Medicine men obtained their powers through visions or dreams in which their familiar spirit revealed itself to them. The Jesuits report that in former times a man who wished to become an *arendiwane* fasted in seclusion for an entire month. During this time he saw no one except an assistant who brought him provisions and who likewise fasted. Even at the time the reports were written prolonged fasting and the avoidance of sexual contact were necessary to become a medicine man. Some medicine men claimed a supernatural origin for themselves. Tonneraouanont, one of the famous medicine men of the Attignawantan, was a small hunchback who claimed that he was a spirit that had decided to become a man. He left the subterranean abode where he had been living and entered the womb of the first woman he encountered. The woman, knowing that the child she bore had not been conceived by human means, induced an abortion. Then she wrapped the living fetus in a beaver skin and abandoned it in the hollow of a tree. When a man passed by, the fetus cried out and the man carried it back to the village, where the mother was able to adopt it. Tonneraouanont claimed that when he was still young, he caused several children to die because they had ridiculed his physical condition. This self-identification of a hunchback with a spirit was easy for the Huron to accept, because they pictured a number of their important mythological beings, including the god of war, as dwarfs.

Satisfying Soul Desires

The Huron attempted to satisfy soul desires both to avoid and cure illness. Soul desires were, for the most part, a request by an individual for something he did not have; hence, they could be satisfied only by someone else. Since the health and well-being of fellow villagers was at stake, the Huron felt obliged to help people, insofar as this was possible, satisfy their soul desires. Some desires, however, were impossible to satisfy in the form in which they were asked, either because the things that were requested could not be obtained or because the desire itself was destructive toward the asker or toward other people. Because the desires that were expressed and the ways in which they were satisfied were subject to social control, an investigation of this area of behavior reveals many interesting features of Huron culture.

We are told that often when a medicine man believed his patient was beyond recovery, he would suggest that his soul desired things that he knew were impossible to obtain. In these cases the man's death was attributed to the failure to satisfy his inner wishes. In many cases, however, it was believed possible to substitute items that were cheaper or more easily obtainable for those that had been suggested. In one case, for example, a mother dreamed that if her son was to become well, he had to receive one-hundred cakes of tobacco and four beaver skins. In place of this he was given ten cakes of tobacco and four large fish. In this way, individuals were dissuaded from making selfish and exhorbitant demands upon the community or from using the institution as a means of self-aggrandizement. Substitution was also used to protect individuals. A desire to commit an act of violence might be fulfilled symbolically. We have already noted the case of a warrior who dreamed he would be captured and burned at the stake. To avoid this he had his fellow villagers go through the preliminaries of torturing him, but a dog was killed in his place. In such ways, the community was able to keep the destructive tendencies of soul desires under careful control.

Very often, when people were sick, various ceremonies were seen as necessary to satisfy the wishes of their souls. While anyone had the right to expect the community to show concern for his or her welfare, ceremonies involving the participation of the whole village appear to have been performed only for the wealthier and more prominent families who could provide food and presents for the participants. Often the curing ceremonies were highly stereotyped. In order to heal a particular person, a certain healing society might be seen as required to perform its rituals or a ceremony such as the *Ononharoia* might be requested. Feasts involving the entire village had to receive the approval of the village council.

On account of dreams, many personal variations were introduced into these rituals. One woman, who seems to have been suffering from a kind of nervous disorder, claimed that when she went out of her house one night, the moon appeared to her as a beautiful tall woman (Aataentsic?) who ordered that all the surrounding tribes should offer the woman the distinctive products of their region. The moon also commanded that ceremonies be held in the woman's honor and that she dress in red. This was to be done so she would resemble the moon, which was made of fire. When she returned home, the woman became giddy and suffered from severe muscular spasms. As a result of all this, it was decided that the *Ononharoia* should be performed for her. Since she was not living in the community where she had been born (another hint that residence was not always matrilocal), the chiefs of her natal village were asked to have this ceremony performed for her. They agreed, and the woman was carried to that village in a basket, accompanied by twenty or thirty singing persons. When she arrived, she was approached by two men and two girls wearing special costumes and was asked what she desired. She named twenty-two presents, which the villagers hastened to provide for her.

The chiefs then announced that everyone should keep their fires burning that evening and said that the patient had requested that they should be as large and bright as possible. After sunset, her muscles relaxed so that she could walk. Supported by two people she walked down the middle of every house in the village, in the course of which she passed through (or appeared to pass through) the middle of several hundred fires. In spite of this, she claimed that she felt little if any warmth. After this the *Ononharoia* began. People painted themselves and ran through the village tossing furniture about, breaking pots, and knocking down dogs. For the next three days, these same people had their dreams guessed. On the third day, the woman went through the houses again accompanied silently by a crowd of people. During this part of the ceremony whoever was not accompanying her was supposed to remain indoors. In each house she gave hints in the form of riddles concerning a last desire, which when it was finally guessed was an occasion for great rejoicing. She returned to all the houses a third time to thank everyone for her recovery, which it was believed must inevitably follow. Then a village council was held at which the chiefs reviewed what had happened and gave the woman a final present. This marked the end of the ceremony. In this instance we can see the regular observances of the *Ononharoia* being embroidered to meet the particular wishes of the individual for whom it was being held. Such inventiveness not only increased the interest and variety of these feasts but it also seems to have played an important part in the development of Huron ritual. This area of Huron culture was not regarded as a static and highly formalized one, but was vibrant and creative. Ideas borrowed from other tribes and personal innovations both appear to have played an important role in modifying current practice.

The dog feast was sometimes requested by a patient or recommended by a shaman as a cure for illness. Since the dog that was killed and eaten in this ritual frequently, if not always, was regarded as a substitute for a human being, there appears to have been a strong degree of symbolism in this observance, the dog serving as a substitute for the sick person. In the case of a young man afflicted by madness, two dogs were killed, one of which was especially dear to him.

Prescribing the details of curing ceremonies gave the sick person a certain measure of control over others. He might dream, for example, that all his guests should enter by one door or pass on only one side of the fire. Sometimes the guests were ordered not to touch one another. Failure to observe these rules would impair or destroy the efficacy of the rite being performed.

Some of these controls were of a more or less overtly sexual nature. When the young people of a village were asked to dance for the recovery of someone, they were often told how they should dress and paint themselves. It was also determined by the sick person or his shaman whether they should wear breech-cloths or dance completely naked. At "eat all" feasts the guests were required to eat all the food that was provided, even though they might have to vomit up what they had eaten in order to finish the meal. Guests attending such feasts were not permitted to leave until they had eaten all the food that was provided. At another kind of curing ceremony the guests were asked to eat *andataroni* or bran biscuits, which produced a great deal of stomach gas. It was believed that anyone who broke wind at this ceremony would die. In another instance a woman dreamed that she would be cured if all the young men and women danced naked in her presence and one of the men urinated in her mouth. This ceremony was performed as she requested.

The most sensational of the curing rituals of this nature was the *andacwander*, a public mating of men and women. This was a ceremony that seems to have been desired mainly by old men and women. For one performance all the young, unmarried girls in a village assembled in a sick woman's house and each was asked in turn with which young man she wished to sleep. The men who were selected were notified by the chiefs who were in charge of the ceremony and came the next night to the woman's cabin to sleep with the girls who had chosen them. They occupied the entire house from one end to the other and stayed there until dawn. Throughout the night the sick woman, who was propped up at one end of the longhouse, watched the ceremony while two chiefs (medicine men?), stationed at either end, rattled their tortoiseshells and sang. In the case of an *andacwander* ceremony that was performed for an old man, one girl was chosen to have sexual intercourse with the patient. In spite of the Jesuits' reticence to mention the *andacwander*, it appears to have been a not uncommon ceremony. It is interesting that it was viewed with approval, even though the Huron disapproved of the exhibition of any sort of sexual interest in public. It demonstrates how the Huron used curing rituals to transgress the restrictive norms of their society, albeit in well-defined and short-lived social contexts.

Not all dreams, however, were self-indulgent ones. Sometimes at the *Ononharoia* a rich man dreamed that he was commanded to furnish his house anew. To do this he had to contrive to give away all of his possessions to the people who passed through his house. This search for health through giving conforms with the value the Huron placed on generosity and parallels their custom of giving away property in an effort to avoid becoming the victims of witchcraft.

The Role of Dreams

Not only in sickness but in the normal course of their lives as well dreams played an important role. The Huron paid attention to their dreams when they went hunting, fishing, trading, or when they were at war, as well as in their games, dances, and other celebrations. The Jesuits described dreams as being the principal god of the Huron and the "real masters of the country." The answers to many problems of daily life were deliberately sought in dreams. Because dreams predicted future events and could warn people of dangers that threatened them, the advice of dreams might be followed in preference to that of leading chiefs. Not all dreams were considered to be important, however, and not all were accepted as being true. In general, the public credence given to a dream varied according to an individual's standing in his community. It was said that poor people's dreams counted for little. Likewise, if an individual's dreams were to gain wide credence, he had to prove himself to dream true on a number of occasions.

Wallace (1958) has pointed out that in their concept of soul desires the Huron had achieved a high degree of psychological sophistication. They recognized the conscious and unconscious parts of the mind, knew the force of unconscious longings, and were aware that the frustration of these desires could cause mental and physical illness. Their insistence that an individual was not always able to interpret the true meaning of his dreams also shows that they were aware that desires often express themselves in symbolic forms in dreams. Thus they had noted the distinction between the manifest and latent function of dreams. The Huron considered that the best method to relieve psychic and psychosomatic stress was to satisfy the desire—either symbolically or directly. The other northern Iroquoian cultures held essentially similar ideas about the treatment of such disorders.

Through their dreams the Huron were able to attribute many of their personal frustrations and desires to forces that were not seen as a part of their overt personality or as being subject to conscious control. In a society where there were strong social pressures on the individual to conform, this device provided people with an outlet for their personal feelings. Through their soul desires, individuals who felt neglected, abused, or insecure could make claims upon the community for attention and psychological support.

Wallace has noted that in Huron society men in particular were expected to be independent. In ordinary life they could ask for nothing for fear that in doing so they would compromise their independence and thereby cast doubts on their manliness. Through their dreams, however, they could ask for support and attention without shame. The motivations of women may have been somewhat different. Men were able to distinguish themselves as individuals in war, trade, or politics. A woman might win praise as a good housewife, but the very nature of her work did not leave her with much scope for self-expression. Hence, women may have used their dreams as a means of claiming attention as individuals. In some other parts of the world, spirit possession plays a similar role in making such demands.

In the case of both men and women, soul desires appear to have helped to balance what would otherwise have been a very unequal relationship between the individual and his society. The demands that Huron society made upon the individual for achievement and conformity were balanced by the demands that the individual made for attention and support upon the society as a whole through the medium of his soul desires. From time to time these demands also permitted large numbers of people, whatever their status, to relax the norms of their society and to gratify themselves in ways that were normally impermissible.

The indirect way in which society repaid its debt to the individual is, ironically, further proof of the Hurons' concern for personal dignity. Just as a person could not be overtly coerced, so he could not be openly supported psychologically. To have done so would have been to compromise the Hurons' cherished ideals of personal freedom and independence.

11

A People between Two Worlds

I T IS INCREASINGLY BEING REALIZED that in order to understand the nature of a culture, it is necessary to know how that culture developed. Recent changes in the interpretation of Iroquoian culture history demonstrate the validity of this observation.

Formerly the northern Iroquoians were believed to be a people with a longstanding agricultural tradition who had originated in the southeastern United States and moved into the Northeast only a few centuries before the arrival of the Europeans. Aspects of Iroquois society, such as the calendrical ceremonies that are intimately linked to maize cultivation, were believed to be integral and ancient features of Iroquoian culture. Features of the culture that did not fit into the general southeastern pattern were regarded as a thin veneer that had been adopted from the surrounding Algonkian tribes after the Iroquoians had arrived in the north. Curing societies and the Huron birchbark canoe were interpreted as examples of such borrowings.

It is now clear that the Iroquoian-speaking peoples lived in the Northeast prior to the development of an agricultural economy. These early Iroquoians may have grown some corn, as the Nipissings and Ottawa River Algonkians did in the seventeenth century, but they depended mainly on hunting and gathering. Small bands probably occupied well-defined hunting territories, gathering together in the summer when food was abundant, and scattering in small family groups during the winter. Their political organization would have been appropriately simple and based mainly on kinship. Blood feuds seem to have settled scores between different bands.

After A.D. 1000, the peoples of the Northeast became increasingly reliant upon agriculture and the population increased and tended to cluster in large villages. As society grew more complex, the existing bonds of kinship were reinforced by new ties of reciprocity. Feasts and gift giving played an increasingly important role in Iroquoian life. Among the most important institutions that crosscut the kinship system were the curing societies. Councils on which the clan segments were represented provided political integration, eventually up to the level of the confederacy. As a result of these developments, the indigenous culture of the Northeast was radically transformed. Borrowings, particularly from the southeastern United States, where cultures had arisen that had incorporated many traits of Mesoamerican origin into a new synthesis (Griffin 1966), played a not insignificant role in the development of northern Iroquoian culture. This borrowing was done piecemeal, however, over a long period of time, and the elements were incorporated into a cultural context that was very different from the one from which they had diffused. There is historical evidence that a number of traits, including the blowpipe and the eagle dance, diffused northward or eastward as late as the seventeenth century (Fenton 1940:242). Moreover, at least some of the resemblances between the northern Iroquoian and Mississippian cultures are almost certainly due to independent parallel development. While the cultural development of the Northeast can be viewed as having been influenced by waves of influence from the south, these traits in no way obscure the special features of northern Iroquoian culture.

None of the crops grown in the Northeast was of local origin. Corn, beans, squash, and tobacco had diffused from Mesoamerica by way of the southeastern United States, and the sunflower appears to have been domesticated in the latter region. Throughout all of eastern North America the planting, care, and harvesting of crops were female occupations, and it seems that this pattern too diffused from the Southeast. It is less certain whether the matrilineal features of Iroquoian society are of southeastern origin. These features might have developed independently in the Northeast as a response to shifts in the subsistence pattern.

There is growing archaeological evidence that the Iroquian longhouse evolved gradually in the Northeast. While some architectural principles of southeastern derivation may have been involved, the basic principles of the Huron longhouse appear to be derived from a house-building tradition of long standing in the north. None of the Iroquoian tribes adopted the rectangular wattle-and-daub houses, the platform mounds, or the formal plazas that are features of Mississippian culture.

Also lacking are the elaborate pottery traditions of the southeastern cultures, with their many vessel forms and elaborate techniques of decoration. The Iroquoians, like their Algonkian neighbors, were content to manufacture only one functional kind of ceramic vessel, one of rather poor quality. Also absent are the design elements of the southeastern ceremonial complex (southern cult), that were associated with Mississippian culture.

In the spheres of politics and religion more southeastern and Mesoamerican influences can be noted, although the differences remain greater than the similarities. The distinction between peace chiefs and war chiefs was general in the Southeast (Driver 1961:340), and at least the basic idea underlying this feature of Huron political organization may be of southern origin. Traces of a similar principle can be seen in the city states of Mesoamerica. Among the Aztec, for example, the two leading officials were the "chief of men," who represented the nation in foreign affairs, and the "snake woman," a man who was in charge of the temples and rituals of the nation. In Mexico, however, the war chief had acquired far greater powers than his civil counterpart. The lack of a detailed similarity with any southern culture suggests that whatever southern influences there were were of a general rather than a specific nature.

The calendrical ceremonies that play such an important role in Morgan's description of the Iroquois also appear to have been inspired by similar agricultural ceremonies in the Southeast. There is, however, evidence to suggest that these celebrations were not an important part of the northern Iroquoian culture pattern until long after the downfall of the Huron.

In customs associated with warfare and human sacrifice clear parallels can be found with those of the southeastern United States and Mesoamerica. The specific similarities include the sacrifice of prisoners, the removal of the heart, the killing of the victim on an elevated platform and in view of the sun, and the cooking and eating of all or part of his body. The Aztec, with their elaborate civilization, waged war for economic gain and had developed a complex metaphysical rationale for human sacrifice, which was believed necessary to strengthen their gods and preserve the world from destruction. The greater primitiveness of the North American cultures is evident in the importance that they attached to blood revenge and the degree to which this theme permeated the slaughtering of prisoners. Moreover, the Aztec practiced retainer sacrifice, slaves being killed to serve their masters after death. Retainer sacrifice was also known in the southeastern United States, but was inconceivable within the context of northern Iroquoian culture. Nevertheless, in spite of the great differences in social structure and levels of cultural development that separate the Huron and the Aztec, both appear to have shared certain elements of a sacrificial complex that were derived from a common source.

The Iroquoian tendency to attach religious significance to many of their games may also be the result of ideas that were ultimately of Mesoamerican origin. Evidence of Mesoamerican influence is stronger in the Southeast, where playing fields were attached to many villages. Although ball games were an important element in Mesoamerican culture, the game of lacrosse has no parallels in Mexico and appears to have originated in the Northeast (Swanton 1946:674).

In spite of these southern influences, Huron and Iroquoian society generally was an indigenous development. The clearly marked social stratification that prevailed among southeastern tribes such as the Natchez not only was absent in the north but was alien to Iroquoian values. Respect for the autonomy of the clan segment remained the keystone of Iroquoian social and political organization. This remained the case even among the Huron whose trading orientation and dense concentration of settlement probably generated more pressures against this principle than existed among any other group in the Northeast in the first half of the seventeenth century.

A concern for the disposal of the dead had been a persistent focus of interest in the Northeast. Hence it is not surprising that the most distinctive feature of Huron culture was their burial rites. These clearly marked the culmination of developments that were an integral part of Ontario Iroquoian culture history. The rites that were associated with the construction of ossuaries had become a ceremony designed to reinforce the solidarity of the Huron confederacy and the ties between the Huron and their northern trading partners. The importance of these ceremonies seems to reflect the unparalleled geographical proximity that had been achieved by the Huron tribes as well as the extreme degree to which the Huron had come to depend on trade. Both of these developments were made possible by the unique location of Huronia in rich farmland near the edge of the Canadian shield.

In summary, it is clear that increasing dependence on horticulture brought about many changes among the northern Iroquoian-speaking peoples. Some of these resulted from internal development, others from external influences that the new economy had allowed to penetrate the region for the first time. In the process of cultural change, the Iroquoians had shown themselves to be good handymen, using whatever ideas were at hand to adapt to changing conditions. It is also clear, however, that the influences of an older hunting and gathering way of life remained strong. One example of this is the shamanistic curing societies which were clearly an old institution that had found a new role for itself in an evolved social order.

It is also clear that in spite of the generally healthy condition of Iroquoian culture, most of the basic tensions that did exist resulted from unresolved contradictions between the old and new ways of life. This is seen clearly in the relations between the sexes and the efforts of men, who had formerly played a major role as hunters, to acquire individual prestige under new conditions. These efforts explain, at least in part, the interest in raiding that was shared by the agricultural tribes in this region.

Iroquoian society cannot be viewed as having a totally integrated culture pattern, but instead must be seen as a series of societies in the process of evolving from a hunting-and-gathering way of life to a horticultural one. Although we know little about the precise rates of change in Huron and Iroquois cultures, it seems that in some aspects of material culture (such as village fortifications) the Huron were at a more primitive stage of development than were the Iroquois. This is to be expected from their geographical location. However, the unique location of the Huron on the northernmost limits of effective corn agriculture led to an interaction with the northern hunters that permitted them to achieve an unparalleled development in other aspects of their culture. The Huron may be seen, from both a geographical and a developmental point of view, as a people living between two worlds.

Matriarchal and Conservative Tendencies

One of the interesting features of our information about the Huron is its failure to provide anything parallel to Morgan's picture of the importance of matrilineal institutions among the Iroquois or to his emphasis on the important role played by women in Iroquois society. Among the Huron, offices and apparently clan membership descended through the female line. Yet, even when we make allowances for the failure of the French to understand Huron customs, in only a very few cases do references to postnuptial residence patterns suggest that it was normally with the wife's family. Moreover, clearcut cases of other extended family residence patterns are recorded. This challenges the traditional picture of the Huron household as being focused on a woman and her daughters. Moreover, while women may have exerted considerable influence over their daughters and in the home, there is no evidence that they exercised any significant political power. If they had, it seems likely that the French would have noticed it. The higher penalities that were prescribed by Huron law for killing a woman do not indicate that women necessarily occupied a privileged position in Huron society; they may simply have been, as the Huron said, recognition that women were less able to defend themselves. While Huron women clearly were not subject to male domination, no one reading the French accounts would assign them a pre-eminent role in Huron society.

It is possible that the role of women among the Huron was different from what it was among the Iroquois. Perhaps because the Huron were a more northerly group, the status of women was less affected among them by the development of a horticultural economy than it had been among the Iroquois. However, it should be noted that Cara Richard's (1967) study of patterns of residence among the Iroquois in the seventeenth century also fails to confirm Morgan's view of the importance of uxorilocal residence among the five nations. This suggests that the role of women in Iroquois society may have been enhanced sometime after the period we are discussing. This may have started with the wars that the Iroquois fought with their neighbors over the control of the fur trade. With a growing emphasis on war, woman may have come to play an increasingly important role in the domestic affairs of the confederacy. Such a development is not uncommon in militaristic societies. Later, as the Iroquois fell increasingly under European domination, the importance of men declined as trade and warfare ceased to be important and as they were compelled to make a not very successful adaptation to European methods of farming. These developments undoubtedly further enhanced the role of women in Iroquois society. It seems clear that Iroquoian women were more conservative than men. Possibly this was because women remained in their villages and therefore identified more closely with the customs of their community than the men did. The latter traveled, met other tribes, and therefore were more exposed to different ways of life. As a conservative and increasingly important influence in Iroquois life, women undoubtedly tended to idealize and exaggerate the role they had played in traditional Iroquoian society. In this fashion, the vision of the aboriginal Iroquoians as a "matriarchal" people was created.

These developments, however, raise some further questions about the alleged conservatism of Iroquoian culture as a whole. Ethnologists who are impressed by the persistence of native traits in present-day Iroquois culture attribute this to the conservatism of the Iroquois. Wright (1966:99, 100) has attempted to project this conservatism into the past, arguing that without such a cultural emphasis the archaeological materials would not lend themselves so easily to the detailed reconstruction of Iroquoian culture history. It should be noted, however, that the archaeological record consists of a limited range of material culture, for the most part pottery. Important as pottery may be for the archaeologist,

DOBYNS, HENRY F., 1966, Estimating Aboriginal American Population. *Current Anthropology* 7:395–449.

DRIVER, HAROLD E., 1961, *Indians of North America.* Chicago: University of Chicago Press.

EGGAN, FRED, 1966, *The American Indian: Perspectives for the Study of Social Change.* London: Weidenfeld and Nicolson.

FENTON, WILLIAM N., 1940, Problems Arising from the Historic Northeastern Position of the Iroquois. Washington: *Smithsonian Miscellaneous Collections* 100:159–252.

———, 1951, Locality as a Basic Factor in the Development of Iroquois Social Structure. Washington: *Bureau of American Ethnology,* Bulletin 149:35–54.

GRIFFIN, JAMES B., 1966, Mesoamerica and the Eastern United States in Prehistoric Times. Robert Wauchope (general ed.), *Handbook of Middle American Indians,* Vol. 4:111–131. Austin: University of Texas Press.

HEIDENREICH, CONRAD E., 1966, Maps Relating to the First Half of the 17th Century and their Use in Determining the Location of Jesuit Missions in Huronia. *The Cartographer* 3:103–126.

———, 1967, The Indian Occupance of Huronia 1600–1650. R. Louis Gentilcore (ed.), *Canada's Changing Geography:* 15–29. Scarborough, Ontario: Prentice-Hall of Canada, Ltd.

HERMAN, MARY W., 1956, The Social Aspects of Huron Property. *American Anthropologist* 58:1044–1058.

HICKERSON, HAROLD, 1960, The Feast of the Dead among the Seventeenth Century Algonkians of the Upper Great Lakes. *American Anthropologist* 62:81–107.

HOFFMAN, D. W., R. E. WICKLUND, and N. R. RICHARDS, 1962, *Soil Survey of Simcoe County, Ontario.* Ottawa and Guelph: Ontario Soil Survey Report No. 29.

HUNT, GEORGE T., 1940, *The Wars of the Iroquois: a Study in Intertribal Trade Relations.* Madison: University of Wisconsin Press.

HUNTER, ANDREW F., 1899, Notes on Sites of Huron Villages in the Township of Tiny, Simcoe County. Toronto: *Annual Archaeological Report,* 1898.

———, 1900, Notes on Sites of Huron Villages in the Township of Tay, Simcoe County. Toronto: *Annual Archaeological Report,* 1899:51–82.

———, 1902, Notes on Sites of Huron Villages in the Township of Medonte, Simcoe County. Toronto: *Annual Archaeological Report,* 1901:56–100.

———, 1903, Notes on Sites of Huron Villages in the Township of Oro, Simcoe County. Toronto: *Annual Archaeological Report,* 1902:153–183.

———, 1904, Indian Village Sites in North and South Orillia Townships. Toronto: *Annual Archaeological Report* 1903:105–125.

JONES, ARTHUR E., 1908, *"Wendake Ehen,"* or *Old Huronia.* Toronto: Report of the Bureau of Archives for the Province of Ontario, V:1–505.

KIDD, KENNETH E., 1949, *The Excavation of Ste. Marie I.* Toronto: University of Toronto Press.

———, 1952, Sixty Years of Ontario Archeology. James B. Griffin (ed.), *Archeology of the Eastern United States,* pp. 71–97. Chicago: University of Chicago Press.

———, 1953, Excavation and Historical Identification of a Huron Ossuary. *American Antiquity* 18:359–379.

KNOWLES, NATHANIEL, 1940, The Torture of Captives by the Indians of Eastern North America. Philadelphia: *Proceedings of the American Philosophical Society* 82:151–225.

KROEBER, A. L., 1939, *Cultural and Natural Areas of North America.* Berkeley: University of California Press.

LOUNSBURY, FLOYD G., 1961, Iroquois-Cherokee Linguistic Relations. William N. Fenton and John Gulick (eds.), *Symposium on Cherokee and Iroquois Culture,* pp. 11–17. Washington: Bureau of American Ethnology, Bulletin No. 180.

MACNEISH, RICHARD S., 1952, *Iroquois Pottery Types.* Ottawa: National Museum of Canada, Bulletin No. 124.

McPHERRON, ALAN, 1967, On the Sociology of Ceramics: Pottery Style Clustering, Marital Residence, and Cultural Adaptations of the Algonkian-Iroquoian Border. Elisabeth Tooker (ed.), *Iroquois Culture, History and Prehistory*, pp. 101–107. Albany: The University of the State of New York.

MORGAN, LEWIS H., 1871, *Systems of Consanguinity and Affinity of the Human Family.* Washington: Smithsonian Contributions to Knowledge, Vol. 17.

OTTERBEIN, KEITH F., 1964, Why the Iroquois Won: An Analysis of Iroquois Military Tactics. *Ethnohistory* 11:56–63.

POPHAM, ROBERT E., 1950, Late Huron Occupations of Ontario: An Archaeological Survey of Innisfil Township. *Ontario History* 42:81–90.

QUAIN, BUELL, 1937, The Iroquois. Margaret Mead (ed.), *Cooperation and Competition among Primitive Peoples.* pp. 240–281. New York: McGraw-Hill, Inc.

RANDS, ROBERT L., and CARROLL L. RILEY, 1958, Diffusion and Discontinuous Distribution. *American Anthropologist* 60:274–297.

RIDLEY, FRANK, 1954, The Frank Bay Site, Lake Nipissing, Ontario. *American Antiquity* 20:40–50.

———, 1961, *Archaeology of the Neutral Indians.* Port Credit Ontario: Etobicoke Historical Society.

RICHARDS, CARA, 1967, Huron and Iroquois Residence Patterns 1600–1650. Elisabeth Tooker (ed.), *Iroquois Culture, History and Prehistory*, pp. 51–56. Albany: The University of the State of New York.

SCHNEIDER, DAVID M., and KATHLEEN GOUGH, 1961. *Matrilineal Kinship.* Berkeley and Los Angeles: University of California Press.

SWANTON, J. R., 1946, *The Indians of the Southeastern United States.* Washington: Bureau of American Ethnology, Bulletin No. 137.

TOOKER, ELISABETH, 1960, Three Aspects of Northern Iroquoian Culture Change. *Pennsylvania Archaeologist* 30:65–71.

———, 1963, The Iroquois Defeat of the Huron: A Review of Causes. *Pennsylvania Archaeologist* 33:115–123.

———, 1968, Sibs, Clans, Gentes, Tribes, Nations and Related Matters. *Bulletin of the Philadelphia Anthropological Society* 19, No. 2:14–17.

TRIGGER, BRUCE G., 1960, The Destruction of Huronia: A Study in Economic and Cultural Change, 1609–1650. *Transactions of the Royal Canadian Institute* 33, No. 68, Pt. 1:14–45.

———, 1962, The Historic Location of the Hurons. *Ontario History* 54:137–148.

———, 1963a, Settlement as an Aspect of Iroquoian Adaptation at the time of Contact. *American Anthropologist* 65:86–101.

———, 1963b, Order and Freedom in Huron Society. *Anthropologica* N.S. 5:151–169.

———, 1965, The Jesuits and the Fur Trade. *Ethnohistory* 12:30–53.

———, 1967, Settlement Archaeology—Its Goals and Promise. *American Antiquity* 32:149–160.

———, 1968, The French Presence in Huronia: The Structure of Franco-Huron Relations in the First Half of the Seventeenth Century. *The Canadian Historical Review* 49:107–141.

WALLACE, ANTHONY, F. C., 1958, Dreams and the Wishes of the Soul: A Type of Psychoanalytic Theory among the Seventeenth Century Iroquois. *American Anthropologist* 60:234–248.

WILSON, DANIEL, 1885, The Huron-Iroquois of Canada, a Typical Race of American Aborigines. Ottawa: *Proceedings and Transactions of the Royal Society of Canada*, Series I, Vol. 2, Sect. 2:55–106.

WITTHOFT, JOHN, 1959, The Ancestry of the Susquehannocks. John Witthoft and W. F. Kinsey III, (eds.), *Susquehannock Miscellany.* pp. 19–60. Harrisburg: The Pennsylvania Historical and Museum Commission.

WRIGHT, JAMES V., 1966, *The Ontario Iroquois Tradition.* Ottawa: National Museum of Canada, Bulletin No. 210.

Recommended Reading

The most important readings are Kinietz 1940 and Tooker 1964.

FENTON, WILLIAM N., 1940, Problems Arising from the Historic Northeastern Position of the Iroquois. Washington, D.C.: *Smithsonian Miscellaneous Collections* 100:159–252.

Although written prior to the development of the *in situ* theory of Iroquoian origins, this paper remains the best general survey of northern Iroquoian culture.

HICKERSON, HAROLD, 1962, *The Southwestern Chippewa: an Ethnohistorical Study.* Menasha, Wisc.: American Anthropological Association, Memoir No. 92.

A revolutionary study of the changes brought about in the social organization of the Ojibwa now living at the western end of Lake Superior as a result of European contact and the fur trade. Important for understanding the Hurons' northern neighbors.

HUNT, GEORGE T., 1940, *The Wars of the Iroquois: a Study in Intertribal Trade Relations.* Madison: University of Wisconsin Press.

A now classic study of the impact of the fur trade upon relations among the tribes of northeastern North America. However, Hunt's use of his sources often leaves much to be desired.

JURY, WILFRED, and ELSIE M. JURY, 1954, *Sainte-Marie among the Hurons.* Toronto: Oxford University Press.

An excellent study of the Jesuits' efforts to introduce various aspects of European culture among the Huron between 1639 and 1649.

KINIETZ, W. VERNON, 1940, *The Indians of the Western Great Lakes, 1615–1760.* Ann Arbor: University of Michigan Press.

A valuable summary of historical data concerning the Huron and a number of Algonkian tribes around the western Great Lakes. Interesting discussions. Less detailed information about the Huron than in Tooker.

MORGAN, LEWIS H., 1954, *League of the Ho-dé-no-sau-nee or Iroquois.* New Haven: Human Relations Area Files (reprint) (originally published 1851).

A description of Iroquois culture based on Morgan's fieldwork in the first half of the nineteenth century. An anthropological classic.

PARKMAN, FRANCIS, 1867, *The Jesuits in North America in the Seventeenth Century.* Boston: Little, Brown & Company.

An erudite account of French-Huron relations written from the viewpoint of a protestant American. A classic of nineteenth century Americana.

SHIMONY, ANNEMARIE A., 1961, *Conservatism among the Iroquois at the Six Nations Reserve.* New Haven: Yale University Publications in Anthropology, No. 65.

A study of the traditional culture of the Iroquois presently living at the Six Nations reserve in Ontario.

SPENCER, ROBERT F., JESSE D. JENNINGS, *et al.,* 1965, *The Native Americans.* New York: Harper & Row, Publishers.

A general survey of the prehistory and ethnology of the North American Indians. Useful for noting the broad distribution of the basic features of Huron culture.

TOOKER, ELISABETH, 1964, *An Ethnography of the Huron Indians, 1615–1649.* Washington, D.C.: Bureau of American Ethnology, Bulletin No. 190.

This principal source book for the study of the Huron presents a carefully organized paraphrase of all the data about them contained in the writings of Champlain, Sagard, and the Jesuit *Relations,* along with notes comparing these data with Iroquois and Wyandot culture.

WRIGHT, JAMES V., 1966, *The Ontario Iroquois Tradition.* Ottawa: National Museum of Canada, Bulletin No. 210.

A synthesis of archaeological data pertaining to the development of Iroquoian culture in Ontario. Useful for the light it sheds on Huron prehistory.